SAILING BARGE VENTA

SAILING BARGE VENTA

LONDON - STOCKHOLM - LONDON
1964 - 1966

A UNIQUE JOURNEY

COMPILED BY JOHN FAIRBROTHER & JOCELYN LUKINS

Cover photograph: from an original by David McGregor

Endpaper maps: © Janet Harker

Frontispiece: VENTA off Isle of Wight. Courtesy Beken of Cowes 1928 ©

Title page colour photo: Tony and John stowing VENTA's mizzen

VENTA plans: ©Tony Smith

Production and design by Jean Goodwin

Printed and bound in Great Britain by J. Thomson Colour Printers, Glasgow

Published by Venta books
in association with
Chaffcutter Books

www.chaffcutter.com

The majority of photographs are by Jocelyn Lukins who would like to
thank the following for additional ones:

John Fairbrother, Nicholas Hardinge, Eva Larsson, Paddy O'Driscoll,
David McGregor, Richard Sadler, Tessa Trager & Richard Walsh

ISBN 978-0-9576437-0-3

**In memory of Jocelyn Lukins 1929-2014
who sadly died before this book was
published.**

THE AUTHORS

SKIPPER JOHN FAIRBROTHER

Born 1930. His father, a doctor in Hampstead. John was sent to a prep school at Brackley, Northants at the tender age of 8½ where he 'survived' until going in 1944 to Bryanston, Dorset where he 'only lasted two years.' Then to Enfield Technical college.

Seeing a photo of the PARMIR bound for London in a newspaper "changed my life. I didn't manage to get on the PARMIR or VIKING that arrived soon after, so it became barges." In 1948 he became 3rd hand on the SPINAWAY C and GLADYS and then moved rapidly on to become Mate on the ETHEL, MAY and FELIX.

He was skipper of the SPINAWAY C at 21, in command of steel barge REPERTOR from 1952-54 and from 1954-58 skipper of the SPINAWAY C for Cranfields, taking grain from London to Ipswich. His fastest passage from London-Ipswich was 12 hours.

Sailed MEMORY for the Sailing Barge Preservation Society from July 1959-Feb 1960, then a year in Cork harbour, Ireland and Skipper of the REMERCIE.

Worked as stonemason on Gloucester and Canterbury Cathedrals until 1963.

Sailed VENTA to Sweden 1964 and back to Maldon in 1966.

Owner Skipper of KITTY in Charter Work 1964 -1976.

Throughout this book the skipper's log is set on a tinted background. The rest is Jocelyn's commentary.

JOCELYN LUKINS

Born Somerset but has spent most of her life in London. She became a photographer and later an antique dealer, and later still combined the two in producing ten reference books on the subject.

This developed into publishing other subjects including this one and part owning and publishing a magazine 'Collecting Doulton'. Combining the whole with owning, living on and chartering two boats for twenty years.

VENTA PLANS

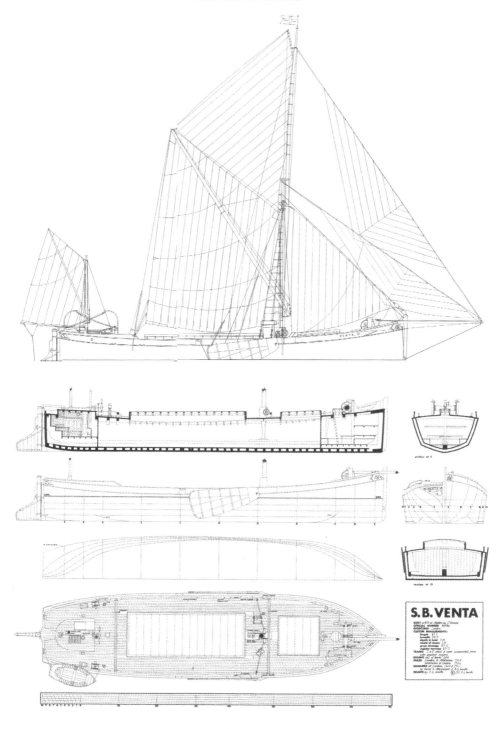

S.B. VENTA

Forward by skipper John Fairbrother

I don't know how many of you who read this have ever sailed in a barge. The facts that set them apart from most other sailing craft are their size and that they are flat bottomed which makes them totally unsuitable for really going to sea. I am well aware that they did work down channel and to nearer continental ports. Some men in them were undoubtedly hard cases and drove their barges hard, but to do it they drove themselves harder. After the Second World War the sailing trade ceased down channel but even on the Essex and Suffolk coasts there have been some real hard cases and several barges were lost.

I have never worked the channel but it must have involved, long, long waits for suitable weather in order to make the next good anchorage or harbour, which is not made much of in books. A barge's flat bottom gives her stability to sail without ballast; this is the reason, as well as her famous ability to be sailed by two men, she has outworked all other sailing craft on the coast or sea, come to that. It also means she doesn't draw much water, hence leeboards. A light barge, of these I write, only requires a very moderate swell before she begins to pound each time she comes down on the water. It might as well be a brick wall it as slows her down and can easily make winding (tracking) difficult; not to mention that the more she is knocked about the more the crew will have to pump out. A round bottomed vessel under sail does not lift clear of the water or offer such large flat surfaces to it. Leeboards themselves are at risk at sea, having just winded a barge when there is swell, the weather one can easily be wrenched off by a wave getting inside and under it. The lee one is somewhat safer until the barge starts to jump onto it. This being particularly so in the cases of barges with flared sides.

The sprit is the other hazard of barging at sea, at all times it must be held in the desired position by the rolling vangs. The lee one only is used, it leading from the sprit end outside all the rigging and made fast with a fall as large as the vangs proper, on the bluff of the bow. The best way to see that there is no movement of the sprit is to slack the sprit just a bit further off than is really needed - take the rolling vang fall in and make it fast - then put the vang fall on the crab winch barrel and heave it in as tight as possible, making the end fast on a cleat the after side of the crab winch - then lift the pawl on the winch so that the winch does not bear all the weight - and don't forget to put the pawl back. As long as the sprit is not free to roll inboard it will not be able to roll outboard again, which is when it could very soon get broken by the vang, or break the vang if it failed to stop the sprit's outboard motion. A loaded barge at sea will not pound in the same way as a light one.

There is considerable engineering weakness in the rectangular section of a barge, largely made up for by massive construction. A light barge concentrates all weight down through the sides to the chine, while the upward thrust of the water is all over the bottom. In a barge there is nothing to hold the bottom down from the post under the mast to the stern post and it is noticeable that in all barges that are hogged, the hump is in the middle of the main hold, some even show a tendency here to hog from side to side. It is by no means unknown for barges to slack the main rigging when the weight of cargoes re-flattens the bottom or for cabin doors to jam.

This is all somewhat by the way, with regard to my tale except to make it clear, I hope, that barges are not now and never were meant for seagoing. I would not have accepted the offer of sailing VENTA if there had been any time limit set for our arrival in Stockholm and I had every intention that patience and caution would be the orders of the voyage having no taste for adventure, so called, at sea.

The stern line of the VENTA (ex JACHIN) in 1893

8

SAILING BARGE VENTA, Ex JACHIN

1893 Built by John Howard of Maldon, Essex, 'a consummate artist', a coaster named JACHIN for J. Frost & Partners, Southampton and Tollesbury. Harry Stone was one of four partners. "One of the finest ever launched", said skipper Jim Stone, one of eight brothers all working in sailing barges and 'boomies', ketch rigged barges.

Mr Harvey, who as a young shipwright worked on VENTA, recalled when he found a rind gall in a timber in her stem and asked Mr Howard if he should cut it out and fit a piece in. He replied, "No lad, we don't work that way here. Fetch another timber." I believe Howard's became bankrupt eventually, probably due to these high standards but they produced some beautiful vessels with their characteristic fine sheer lines. VENTA was 87' long, 20'8" wide and with a depth of hold of 7'1" and a registered tonnage of 70 tons. Her stern was small and elegant with an almost triangular transom. The skipper's cabin was very fine with its alternate pine and mahogany boards and rose quartz ports. An unusual feature was her round fo'c's'le hatch. Many Howard barges were named for flowers e.g. VIOLET and HYACINTH. JACHIN had lilies carved on her bow badges whilst another, OAK, had oak leaves. The carving was done by one of Howard's sons who was handicapped.

After cabin restored 1960-4

1914   On 14th March of this year when bound for Newport, Isle of Wight with wheat, JACHIN went over a groyne at Newhaven and sustained serious damage. After having tried to enter the harbour in a strong S.W. wind the crew were taken off by the Newhaven lifeboat and the barge was stranded by the east pier. She was abandoned and sank off Seaford, Sussex. The cargo was washed out of her and she was expected to be a total wreck but was later salved. A schooner was wrecked at Newhaven on the same day and towed into the harbour in a sinking condition. JACHIN's wreck was bought by Shrubsall of East Greenwich and rebuilt, doubled and renamed VENTA and taken into their fleet, which were all named for Victoria and Albert with V&A incorporated into the name, i.e. VERONA, VICUNIA, VERONICA, VICTORIA etc. VENTA's port of registry was changed to London and her registered owner was a woman, Miss Elsie Shrubshall.

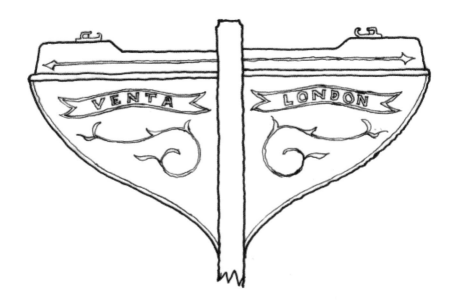

The stern line of the VENTA in 1914

1923   On the 5th of October this year on passage from Rochester, Kent to Torquay, Devon with cement VENTA broke her sprit in heavy weather. The master made for Shoreham, Sussex but wind headed him and he was unable to make port in her crippled state and the barge was driven down past the Isle of Wight. Here she fell in with a Norwegian steamer S.S. ROCH whose skipper agreed to tow her into port but the weather increased and after taking off the crew he slipped the tow S.W. off Beachy Head and landed at Dover.

Abandoned, VENTA drifted for four days until a French trawler towed her into Dieppe. Mr Shrubshall went over to survey the damage and when the hatch covers were taken off he found only one bag of cement was spoiled where a trickle of water had come in at a knee. The barge was towed back to Greenwich on 24.11.1923 to refit.

1926   VENTA's CARGO BOOK (This information was noted by Hervey Benham when serving as mate on VENTA in 1939.)

Skipper William Crosswell Crew - Mate & Boy as 3rd hand		
January	Yarmouth to London	Old rubber
	London to Newport	Wheat
February	Wareham to Battersea	China clay (for Lambeth potteries?)
March	London to Yarmouth	Wheat
April	London to Yarmouth	Wheat
May	Antwerp to Poole	Cement
June	Portland to London	Stone
	Antwerp to Shoreham	Tiles
July	London to Shoreham	Wheat
August	Boom, Belgium to Shoreham	Bricks
September	Neil, Belgium to Isleworth	Bricks
October	London to Poole	Maize
November	Portland Harbour to quay	Coal.
	Portland to Pimlico London	Stone
December	London to Newport	Wheat

Several long trips being made light, two out to Antwerp and return trips from Yarmouth and Shoreham. Time was also expended loading, unloading, waiting for freights and refits. Payment after certain deductions totalled £338 for the year's work. Traditional allowance was: two-thirds of the crew's half for the skipper, one third for the mate. This comprised £4 a week for the skipper, £2 a week for the mate and 2 shillings a day for the boy on passage.

1927 From March this year VENTA made 26 consecutive journeys over 12 months with stone from Cherbourg to Hayling Island and Bosham, Sussex. It is reputed that VENTA and VERAVIA brought stone from Portland, Dorset to London for the building of the Cenotaph in the 1920s.

VERAVIA loading bone meal

Portland Quarries

Discharging flour at St. Peter Port, Guernsey

VERAVIA loaded with wood pulp

1928 Charles Rye joined crew at 16 until 1930.

c 1929 Another freight recorded was one of Portland stone to Wandsworth Bridge, the Fulham side. On this occasion the skipper, the William Cresswell mentioned above, died aboard. George Winn who had the ETHEL EDITH in 1928 and was awaiting a new commission was contacted by his company and asked to go to Ryde and sail the barge to Wandsworth. Our next entry shows that he must have been given the skipper's job after this.

c 1934 Abandoned in English Channel loaded with Portland stone. Her crew and skipper George Winn were picked up by French fishermen and towed into Boulogne. Sold to Harvey of Rochester, Kent.

1939 Skipper Alf Eaglestone of Faversham, described as "a real old coasting skipper" had VENTA at this time. Hervey Benham went as mate with him for six months at the beginning of the Second World War. He said the combination of an elderly skipper and an amateur mate was hard work for him. Hervey was owner of East Coast Newspapers and wrote many definitive books on east coast sailing boats and barges including 'Last Stronghold of Sail' and 'Down Tops'l'.

In the former he published the cargo list for 1926 he found aboard. Hervey later in the year joined the Royal Navy doing coastal patrols off Shoreham, Sussex for the duration.

1930s VENTA working with Francis & Gilders, Colchester fleet.

1947 VENTA sold out of trade to Judge Blagdon, a QC of the High Court as a sailing 'yacht'.

1951 Skipper Fred Cooper, author of 'Handbook of Sailing Barges' and 'Racing Sailormen' skippered and handled the gear from this time. Fred had become master of the GAZELLE at seventeen and was mate in his first barge race aboard GAZELLE in 1927.

1952 Rigged with mainsail and sprit ex ALICE MAY.

Colin Banks amid VENTA's sails, October 1959

1957   Judge Blagdon had 2'3" cut off foot of mainsail for better visibility as he didn't like bending down to see under! Also Fred thought it was to prevent the skipper's delight in knocking off the galley chimneys with the mainsail. Below she had had a 'Whitewall Creek' conversion with small cabins constructed of sheet asbestos!

1959   Lying above the Cathouse at Wolverstone on the river Orwell. Surveyed by P Smith who said, VENTA would be OK as a houseboat "but don't try and sail her". Bought by Jocelyn Lukins on 21.9.59 for £600. The original asking price had been £2000. I only had £500 and borrowed the extra £100 from my friend Nicholas Hardinge. Rigged out at Woolverstone by Nicholas and Fred Wilson, "Nelson", skipper of the VERAVIA and sailed with friends making up the crew from the River Orwell to Greenwich on the Thames. A working barge in trade with an engine, the LADY HELEN had given us a tow through the Spitway.

Fred Wilson and Nicholas Hardinge

Fred and Nicholas rigging out

1959   Moored at Norton's yard, Bugsby's Hole, Greenwich for repairs. Richard Norton had set up business there in 1924. The SERB, SCUD and SCOUT had been built there. Bargemen liked to joke that none of them had a plank of wood of any length in them as the timber had all been retrieved from the Thames.

By this time the workforce had been reduced to one man. Fred lived in a small tarred shed on the river bank which was divided into two parts, his living quarters and the tool store. I never saw inside but my friend, Paddy O'Driscoll told me it was furnished with a let-down pipe cot and a nice little stove which had been removed from a barge's fo'c's'le. It was quite cosy but the mugs were hung on an upright, out of reach of rats which were attracted by the sugar dregs in them! Fuel was retrieved from coal and coke piles in the riverside factory yards and there was unlimited wood of course. Water was available from Dorman Long's works next door. Dorman Long made and installed the high level bridge in Sydney Harbour, Australia. There were no services except a telephone on which visiting barges could ring around for their next cargo. The only access was along the river path.

Twice a day the tide washed the pebble beach. It was a small paradise. I moved down from my Chelsea flat with my cat, Salvador, for company. Salvador was the most superior cat I ever had but he soon mastered the art of getting ashore or aboard at every state of the tide and probably met up with Fred's rats. There was no rent to pay as I was having work done.

'Dicky' Norton was renewing some doubling underneath the barge and Fred was renewing ceiling (floor) inside. One of my friends, Jacqueline Geneau came to lodge, much to Fred's consternation as she floated through the saloon to the bathroom each morning. They didn't see such glamour on the other barges which called at Bugsby's Hole.

The bargemen gave Norton the name of 'Whisper' Norton, because of his loud voice: they always had nicknames for everyone. Whilst I was at Norton's, Nicholas needed a third hand to 'go foreign' on his trading barge, the VERAVIA. It was for a cargo of bricks from Neil in Belgium to Hayling Island in Hampshire. He told me it would take six days and gave me an hour or so to get ready. I left six tins of cat food for Salavador with friends on the ASPHODEL, a nearby barge.

Because of bad weather the journey took six weeks! The crew were skipper 'Nelson', mate Stan Hayward and myself as cook to make up the minimum crew needed by law when crossing the Channel. There couldn't have been a more difficult pair to cook and live with. Nelson had very conservative habits and had to have meat and veg. dinners every day. Rice was 'chink' food, and pasta was 'italiano' grub and Stanley lived on peaches and cream!

The Dutch and Belgium barges we were moored with were as always, very well turned out. Whereas, despite Nicholas's efforts Nelson thought it 'macho' to have his barge in s*** order. While he and Stan went ashore in the evenings I got the paint brushes out and painted the shell bow badges and the rails round and attempted a tidy up. It was a baptism of fire for me, but I passed the test and even enjoyed the trip.

Whilst I was away Nicholas visited the VENTA and one evening he went along the tow path to 'The Pilot' pub, which is still there today dwarfed by the O2 arena. Fred was there drinking alone and Nicholas asked if he could join him. Fred said, "Yes", but added, indicating the others in the bar, "they think me a miserable old bugger, well I am and I likes it that way". At Christmas time I did GPO Christmas post duty along the riverbank and delivered to all the factories which were then thriving there. They were replaced around 2000 with the Millennium housing scheme, much of it designed by an architect who practised from Sweden, Ralph Erskine! There were still rigged working barges passing at this time, such as Cranfield's ANGLIA and MARJORIE, carrying cargoes of wheat from the London Docks to Ipswich with a return cargo of flour. There was very often a convenient return cargo; ashes from London grates were taken to the brick fields and building bricks returned. In years gone by 'Stackies' carried hay for the London horse traffic and 'London mixture', manure was returned to the farms. Nicholas's mother remembers seeing as a child, a small mountain of horse manure at Hyde Park Corner.

Richard Norton , Fred Bayly and 'the shed'

Paddy o' Driscoll visited on moving on day. Here with Jocelyn.

1960 Moored at Cutty Sark Tavern, Greenwich. Went by bus each day to Covent Garden as I had a job at the time at 'The Queen', a society magazine. One of my fellow photographers was a young man, Antony Armstrong Jones. Nicholas had helped him on his first theatre photo-call; for 'Separate Tables'. I was there when his marriage to Princess Margaret took place in Westminster Abbey when his colleagues on 'The Queen' were the official photographers. I spent the day in the darkroom processing all the photographs as they were biked back from the Abbey. Norman Parkinson charmingly congratulated me on my efforts. The mooring proved hard on the barge as the river traffic was very heavy, so we moved on.

Moored on the Thames at Dolphin Square, Victoria, London. Nicholas asked if he could rig VENTA out at his expense and enter her in the 1960 barge races.

23-4-60 Moved to Cubitt's Basin at Chiswick.

14-6-60 VENTA entered the Thames race in the bowsprit class against Everard's racing barges which were stripped for action. Bob Roberts, skipper of our competitors, DREADNOUGHT asked VENTA's skipper Fred "Nelson" Wilson at the start if he was in the 'Pe-aner' class, (piano on board was later buried at sea). Both Ipswich skippers, there had always been rivalry between them.

VENTA completed the course. P Smith the surveyor was one of the judges! Everards had announced that barge racing would cease on the 100th anniversary when they would destroy their fleet and we entered against them in protest. Barge racing continues and with some being rebuilt it seems to have a future. However it is an expensive business today sometimes funded by organisations who have maintenance staff and separate racing crews not like the homespun times we had when those working on them and racing them were very often the same and it was much more fun I'm sure.

A. P. Herbert demonstrates leeboard with a model for the film
'When the Wind Blows', shot at Studio 22, Ealing.

A. P. Herbert came with us on this occasion. He had sailed on Colchester barges at one time and crewed in a barge race. He had done the commentary on a film made by Nicholas on sailing barges 'When the Wind Blows'. He wrote a best-seller 'The Water Gipsies' about narrow boats on the English canals and at this time he was writing a novel about a sailing barge 'The Singing Swan' and came to Chiswick to get information from Nicholas on various details from VENTA until Nicholas said, "Who's writing this book sir, you or I?" It was published in 1968. Sir Alan Herbert was a remarkable man; he was a writer, poet, wit, politician, and author of many comedies. He published numerous articles and books, wrote librettos of operas and many plays. 'The Water Gipsies' and the popular musical 'Bless the Bride' had long runs in the West End.

He was an independent Member of Parliament for Oxford University for 15 years, some of which time he spent in the navy in the Second World War. He became a Freeman of the Company of Watermen and Lightermen of the River Thames. A humourist and a novelist he also did good work in law reform in parliament especially on improving women's lot on divorce. We always saluted him with Tony's trombone when passing his waterfront house at Hammersmith on our way down river each year.

1962   New mainsail by Whitmore of Ipswich, costing then £147.15s.0d.

VENTA entered many of the annual barge races on the Thames, Medway, Blackwater and Orwell through the years. The best positions she achieved were fifth in the Medway and sixth in the Blackwater in 1962 when 'Nelson' won the award for best seamanship around the halfway buoy. She was normally the heaviest barge and although good 'on the straight' lost ground when tacking. VENTA was a heavy coasting barge competing against the nimbler river craft. However we were well turned out and made lots of effort and it was great fun and they were very enjoyable social events.

VENTA's crew were unique in having a uniform in the Hardinge colours, red, black and white. We had various skippers when 'Nelson' was unavailable including Jack Spitty, Bill Blake, 'Tubby' Parter from Faversham, Tommy Baker and William Keddy, all formerly in trade. We were moored on the Thames at Cubitt's Basin, Chiswick. Interior gutted and redesigned in open plan by 'Ark' Tony Smith.

1963 Topsail fitted ex REVIVAL from a suite of racing sails made just before her motorisation and used for only one season. Cost £20. Damage of one mouse-hole repaired by Taylor's of Maldon. We also acquired a kedge anchor ex REVIVAL. The staysail was from FORTIS. It was possible in those days to find second-hand gear which had been abandoned when the sailing barges had engines fitted.

We entered the Blackwater barge race again this year, but were not placed. In a gathering whilst at the Hythe Quay after the race we spoke of the VERONA being in Sweden. Barry Pearce remarked "Wouldn't it be good if the two old gals could meet up?" It was on the strength of this casual remark that we decided to do just that! In those days everything seemed possible. We didn't have much money.

I didn't consider that going that distance spritsail rigged might not be easy which was probably why it had not been done before. VERONA had motored there and other barges which had gone that far to sea had changed to a gaff rig for their journeys. We went back to our mooring at Chiswick and started work making VENTA seaworthy. I quite wrongly thought the Baltic, almost tideless and, shown in my school atlas as almost enclosed, would be a pond. John Fairbrother must have been the one later who considered it could be done and that he would like to try it.

Tony Smith took a rather pedestrian job with Wimpy's, a large building contractor at Hammersmith to earn money for the trip and we both decided we could continue our careers in photography and architecture in Sweden. VENTA's crew worked through the next year with preparations and John Fairbrother came occasionally to Chiswick on a Sunday to see how we were progressing. David Macgregor, marine historian, also came from time to time to photograph the progress.

VENTA and SALTCOTE BELLE at the 3rd Blackwater barge race. 4-6-1964

London - Stockholm - London 1964 to 1966

The Skipper's Introduction

1964 *Early in January 1964, whilst working as a stonemason, sometimes happily, sometimes less so, on the cathedral at Canterbury and wishing there was some prospect of getting back on the water in barges, I received a letter from Jocelyn Lukins, owner of S.B. VENTA. The very next weekend I went to the VENTA's mooring at Chiswick. The barge had its spars in their rightful places though bare of sails. She had only one leeboard shipped and the port quarter covering board and rail were up. I went aboard and was ushered into the very pleasant saloon where lunch was soon served.*

I was introduced to Tony Smith who lived aboard VENTA and Nick Hardinge a frequent visitor. It was then that the idea of sailing VENTA to Stockholm and that I should take her there was discussed. Already a lot of thought had been given to the subject and barging opinions sought as to there being a reasonable chance of VENTA making the passage under sail alone. It was known that VERONA was already at Stockholm but that she had had an engine for the trip.

The route would be through the Kiel Canal. Things like charts, the cost of the Kiel Canal and the preparation of the ship were all talked over at considerable length, although at that time I did not know if I could take the barge. The point of the trip was that Tony and Jocelyn would stay and continue their careers in Sweden and Nick and I, if I went, would stay a short while then return to England.

In the following months I visited VENTA several times and each time found much work had been done. The dinghy had been repaired and the port quarter now looked and in fact was new. The barge had been on the P.L.A. blocks at Strand on the Green and Nick and Tony had completely spiked the bottom. In March I left Canterbury and went to work as a not very good catcher of oysters, still undecided about going to Sweden. However this was settled by the end of May.

John Fairbrother

A replacement Leeboard was acquired from the LORD CHURCHILL and extra anchor chain from HER MAJESTY; two of the barges moored in Cubitt's Basin, which was established in the First World War, when concrete barges were built there to transport ammunition to France. It was now a leafy haven, a community of interesting boats and characters reigned over by Miss Pryce who lived on the HIBERNIA. She had previously lived on the HAUGHTY BELLE a very famous barge which had won many races in the past and was destroyed by a German bomb at Cubitt's during the Second World War. Perhaps it was thought it was still a military establishment.

Cubitt's Yacht Basin, Chiswick moorings.

It was in quite an exclusive community at this time and it was probably Nicholas's aristocratic connections which got us a mooring there outside on the river bank shaded by willow trees; an idyllic rural setting although it did include, across the river, the local sewage farm, crematorium and a graveyard where Sir Richard Burton rested in a replica of an Arabian tent. He was the creator of 'Arabian Nights', not the husband of Elizabeth Taylor. It was picturesque with interesting river traffic and with quite a coterie of 'celebrities' living there, many of them actors and musicians including Arthur Lowe, (Captain Mainwaring of 'Dad's Army' fame), the 'Bonzo do da Band' was formed there, and one of 'The Alberts' lived on a barge there, perhaps now largely forgotten unlike 'The Temperance Seven' who lived in style at Strand on the Green, just up-river

We dressed our mainsail in the Polytechnic Sports Ground 'next door', and their runners' plimsolls turned red with our traditional dressing of red ochre, linseed oil and its secret ingredient. Their boathouse was the terminus of the annual Oxford & Cambridge Boat Race on the Thames and we had a grandstand seat on VENTA for the occasion with parties aboard. Later it became part of a housing development with a small yacht basin, filled with plastic boats and lost all its trees, interesting boats, characters and character.

On VENTA we were all traditionalists and were anxious to carry out the work in the original ways. We all had our different talents. Julian Thompson, who later made delicate architectural models for Ove Arup, one was the Sydney Opera House, was very good at shaping up 5" square pieces of oak at the weekends at Chiswick. Tony Smith had a talent for fine carving and Nicholas learned to splice wire and saw to the rigging. The port covering board, the rail, saddle chock and nibs aft were renewed by the three of them.

It was 'all hands on deck'; my mother made the bob, or house flag, with the Hardinge scallop shells which acted as a wind vane. On its top was the traditional acorn which Nicholas applied with gold leaf. In Norse mythology the god, Thor never strikes his sacred oak tree with lightning, which proved

VENTA leaving P.L.A. blocks at Strand on the Green for Woolwich buoys

to be true. I made a full set of signal flags on my sewing machine. Nicholas and Tony attended a navigation course at the Greenwich Institute.

In April we went upstream to the P.L.A. blocks at Strand on the Green and Nicholas and Tony re-spiked the bottom and hull below the waterline with 7" spikes. Holes had to be bored for them through the doubled bottom and into the 9"x 9"oak frames; hard work lying on your back in the mud.

After repairs and refit the only original Blagdon piece was a light cotton flying spinnaker John Fairbrother named the 'Judge' and when boomed from bowsprit, main or mizzen masts or boom, proved a great asset in light winds and tight corners when sailing to Sweden and back.

4-6-1964 We left Chiswick and were towed down the Thames below bridges to

Waterman Jim Taylor of Bermondsey, who towed VENTA to Woolwich buoys

Woolwich buoys. This was where the working barges tied up and waited for orders. In the depressions, as in the 1930s when work was short, they were known as 'Starvation Buoys'.

Waiting there when we arrived were KIMBERLEY, DANNEBROG, ETHEL, BERIC and CABBY. This group were all former sailing barges fitted now with auxiliary engines: some still had some remnants of sails and spars. Our gear had been lowered to deck level to navigate the bridges and everything formed a heap of ropes ,sails and spars.

Alec Rands of the CABBY, (which was the last full size wooden barge to be built, in 1928) seemed to be the natural 'guv'nor' and everyone set to work without being asked and soon had the gear up. I'm sure they enjoyed every minute. Whilst they were working the BEATRICE MAUD arrived with skipper Harold Smy, 'the last of the sailor-men' who had kept his gear until it almost fell about his ears, as his company would not replace it considering that the days of sail were over.

There should have been a future but its demise was brought about by the London dockers who no longer wanted to negotiate sails and spars with their cranes.

BEATRICE MAUD was one of sixteen barges which went over to Dunkirk in 1940 in a dramatic attempt to bring back our forces who had been fighting in France. Eight of the sixteen didn't come back but others got safely home with cargoes of English and French soldiers.

When our skipper, John Fairbrother, arrived next day at 8 p.m. all was ready to sail although John made continuous alterations to the gear through the next weeks in preparation for our longer journey.

5-6-64 Left Woolwich and our large band of helpers who had obviously enjoyed themselves. Left just before high water with the lights already lit and made fair progress down the river, anchoring near the Yantlet buoy at 3.30 a.m. We left just before high water at 9 a.m., down to and over the Spitway at low water after sailing awhile in company with EDITH MAY, MARJORIE and the SALTCOTE BELLE.

We shaped for Maldon arriving at Hythe Quay before the sun set. VENTA had been built and launched just a few hundred yards upstream from the Hythe. I had not sailed her before this and she gave the impression of being a reliable barge. Several friends visited on board so not much in the way work was done except to try and alter the leech of the topsail which flapped and in fresh winds shook all the gear.

The next month was spent going over VENTA's gear and equipment, in the evenings mainly as most of the crew were still gainfully employed. I even found someone who got me to understand the elements of solar navigation and the use of the sextant.

VENTA had a good patent log, a 20 fathom lead line, compasses, life raft, flares, a fog horn, a motor pump and every possible chart both large and small scale. Several of her running wires were replaced, new ratlines, new rolling vangs and falls with old topmast hoops rigged on the topmast standing back stays to prevent them from catching under the side light boxes. A new bowsprit was made by Nick from an old smack's mast, the SUNBEAM. A perfect, hand-sewn jib made in the 1930s was bought to fit it, the jib's heavy head wire was taken out, to set it flying and replaced with rope and hanks so that it would set on a wire. All the barge's anchor chain was hauled out on deck and the shackles knocked out so they would be free if anything had to be slipped. All was done that could be done to see that the barge was fit for sea. I had never crossed the North Sea or any other sea for that matter and barge sailing at sea was going to be new to me.

| **THE BLACKWATER SAILING BARGE RACE**

9.45 a.m. Set the topsail and left just before high water.

10.30 a.m. Off Southend Pier.

11.15 a.m. Saw another barge under sail off Medway

11.30-11.40 a.m. Measured mile speed 4¾ knots through water.

11.55 a.m. Bore off a little to N. Course now 55 degrees E of N. Mouse buoy ahead.

12.30 p.m. Passed close to Maplin buoy.

3.00 p.m. Crossing the Spitway could touch the bottom with the boathook. Hove log and got 1 fathom and ½ a fathom. Leeboard touched bottom. Sand stirred up in wake.

3.30 p.m. Abreast Clacton Pier. SALTCOTE BELLE to starboard. Touched bottom.

4.25 p.m. Passed close to Knoll buoy.

5.45 p.m. Off Bradwell with EDITH MAY and MARJORIE astern.

6.00 p.m. Race with MARJORIE, she dropped topsail we kept ours and walked away.

6.30 p.m. Took in topsail.

6.45 p.m. Osea Pier. Yacht capsized astern.

7.15 p.m. Heybridge. Rain squalls.

7.30 p.m. Touched bottom. Stayed aground, bow on. MARJORIE, EDITH MAY and SALTCOTE BELLE passed in that order. First two started engines when seeing our plight. Took in all sail except topsail and awaited tide.

8.25 p.m. Moored next to EDITH MAY at Hythe Quay.

'*A WINDWARD START SCORES ON A CALM DAY*

'*From David Fairhall, our Shipping Correspondent.*

'*The weather was almost too good for the Blackwater sailing barge match. A perfect day for a sail if you had nowhere to go, but hardly ever a breeze worthy of these big hulls and heavy brown canvas. However those who spend much time and money keeping these old vessels alive must have been relieved to see every topmast standing at the end of the day.*

'*The match went to the Ipswich barge, MAY. She left most of her rivals standing with a well-judged windward start. Another Ipswich barge SPINAWAY C slipped through the fleet in pursuit but even with the dinghy set as an extra sail, she was still astern when the flood brought them back to Maldon. As if to prove that there is still life in these old boats, VENTA sails this week for Sweden to winter in the ice. Even in the days when big fleets of spritsails could be seen all along the East coast and down channel this would have been an outstanding voyage. The spritsail rig (the sails are brailed up instead of lowered) and leeboards were evolved for efficiency in an estuary strewn with muddy banks and lined with muddy creeks..*

'*WATCHING WEATHER*

'*Mr John Fairbrother, the skipper, will need all his judgement to get her heavy gear and 71 year-old hull to the Baltic in one piece. He has just spent a year or so away from the water working as a stonemason on Canterbury cathedral Now he wants to "have a look at the Swedes". The North Sea crossing does not worry him but he will be watching the weather. "They say a barge'll put up with more than her crew, one man and a boy and 150 tons to sea, but the fact remains a barge was never meant to go to sea, she's got leeboards and a sprit and they could just fall off, if it got nasty."*

'*He added "some luck with the weather and we arrive when we get there." '*

7-6-64 Preparations continued. On Cook's Yard the stern was sheathed with mahogany boards and re-carved and gilded by Tony. The skipper continued his adjustments to the rigging. I shopped both for food and invaluable things like lamp cones and glasses. The only thing which was never used was the salt water soap I had bought at the Army & Navy Stores in Victoria, London, who specialised in fitting out 'expeditions'. The Baltic was almost fresh water and we found facilities to fill our water tanks throughout our route.

5-7-64 Sunday. 1017 millibars. Moderate S.W. wind. SPINAWAY C and VENTURE left 9.30 a.m. Put in new vangs, rolling vangs and topsail sheet.

6-7-64 1016 millibars. High variable wind. Turned out and swung. 8 a.m. MAY towed away, we pulled alongside SALTCOTE BELLE. Set up shroud lanyards. Nicholas and I re-leathered hand pumps. After supper there was a farewell party aboard. Our crew seems to be complete now, Nicholas Hardinge, Tony Smith, Jocelyn and Vernon Gracie. 'Binns' (Barry Pearce) and Ron Hall and quite a few friends from Maldon are coming with us to Harwich. Ron nailed a racehorse shoe on the inside of the stem which came from 'Hardfast'. David Pocknell, a designer friend of Jocelyn's also joined us today.

THE HYTHE MALDON

7-7-64 We had three Barge skippers aboard, John, Barry Pearce and Bill Blake and other experienced crew including Vernon Gracie. I had written to Ralph Erskine in Sweden, the owner of VERONA, to tell him of our plans. He was an internationally renowned architect originally from East Anglia but practicing for many years in Sweden. He had bought VERONA and took her under motor to Stockholm in 1955 to serve as an office. In the summer break the staff sailed off in the barge around the Swedish archipelago. Vernon, an associate who had sailed on VERONA applied to join us for the journey hoping to make it back to England in his three week holiday. He had his own yacht, much faster than VENTA. He didn't tell me of his expectations or I would have warned him that John had only undertaken the journey on the understanding, quite rightly, that he should choose the conditions suitable for a safe passage with no time restrictions. Vernon adapted to our ways and became a lifelong friend.

There was nothing left for me to do today, at least no shopping - everything was aboard, water, gas bottles, paraffin and six months of shopping stowed away. We would have to be self-sufficient for a long while. I paid a farewell visit to Maudie Jay, landlady of 'The Jolly Sailor' and gave her some photographs and an ashtray commemorating the Centennial Barge Match which she loved; in return she gave me some advertising pub trays which came in very handy when serving a sandwich lunch later on deck when we were on our way. We were quite a crowd as more of our Maldon friends joined us for the day's sail. I had lots of help and gifts; Jam from Sonia Norris of LEOFLEDA, marmalade from June Prime of GIPPING, roses from Ron and Janet Hall of the steam tug BRENT and a Baltic guide from Mike & Jackie Hart of RIPPLE.

David MacGregor, sailing craft historian, took advantage of Tommy Hedgecock's launch NELSON which helped us out of the mooring, to film our departure. The result was dramatic; VENTA with all sail set, the sun shining and a fresh breeze. This became the end of a 16mm. film running for 35 minutes that David had made over the months of all the preparations at Chiswick, Woolwich and Maldon. It is now with his records in the GREAT BRITAIN archives at Bristol.

David, being Scottish, was a little miffed at our sailing away and leaving him to pay for the launch. However we were travelling too fast to give him anything but a hearty wave 'Goodbye' and he did get some marvellous photographs.

7-7-64 | 1004 millibars. Freshening W. wind. Bright at first, rain after dark.

We towed clear of Maldon at 11 p.m. with the boat up, the anchor on the bow and bowsprit jib set. By the time we passed Heybridge Lock our launch could no longer keep up with us and we let go and set the bowsprit jib at Mill Beach. We ran down the Wallet and gybed off the Naze. When fetching into Harwich the topsail started to flap on the leach and had to come down, so we turned up the Stour without it to an anchorage above the Gasworks Creek. At 7 p.m. we put our passengers for the day ashore with the help of a small fishing boat. It was quite rough and started to rain soon after.

On their way home to Maldon in the car there was a strong smell of fish and it was found that some very dead crabs had crawled, mysteriously into Barry's pocket.

We had left Hythe Quay at 11 a.m. and the launch at Osea at 12.45 a.m. with a spanking breeze, doing 7¾ knots at one time on the journey. The bowsprit looked fine on its first airing. We came into Harwich at 4 p.m. with a 5 to 6 force wind, very bracing. I had felt a little seasick whilst making the sandwiches as I had not yet got my 'sea legs'. Nicholas was on the pier and said we were a fine sight coming in. He had driven up in one of the cars which was to take our Maldon friends home.

8-7-64 1001 millibars. Strong W. wind. The compass adjuster aboard by 10.30 a.m. We were underway with mainsail and topsail, we made about two boards and gybed twice then went where he directed turning above Parkstone Quay as we had had a brush with the Harbour Master about our manoeuvres and our berth last night. Went ashore.

9-7-64 1007 millibars. Fresh W. Wind. Finished the topsail and though it looks rough it stops the flapping. Ashore to clear for Kiel 10 a.m. Aboard at 1 p.m. Sailed under topsail down to same berth above Harwich by 3 p.m. Water Guard alongside 6 p.m. with clearance and message from David Fairhall, shipping correspondent of *The Guardian* saying he would be on the pier at 10.30 p.m. to join us, which he was. Got him aboard and boat up and after hearing the midnight weather forecast at H W. Got underway.

I had gone ashore and found Parkstone, like Harwich very run down at that time. It had obviously been quite a grand town in the past and had wonderful neglected old houses just asking to be restored, but meanwhile a depressing sight for anyone landing there. The tumbledown ships store could not arrange our bonded store, some cases of 'Grouse' whisky, in less than a week! The skipper was certainly not going to delay our start because of that, probably visualising a drunken crew. However it was put aboard later that day. We were rather short of money for the trip and the whisky was very valuable currency, especially in Sweden to pay for tows and help along the way. Boxing the compass at Harwich in rough weather was difficult as instructions from the adjuster caused VENTA to complete manoeuvres which broke all the rules of right of way. Out rushed the harbour master in his launch to ask why we had not asked his permission and instructing us to moor at Parkstone Quay.

Harbour Master's Office,
Town Hall,
Harwich

HARBOUR MASTER
EUT.-COM. A. WATERS
R.D., R.N.R.

8th. July, 1964.

PHONE: HARWICH 3257

Jocelyn M. Lukins Esq.,
S/B "VENTA",
Cubitt's Yacht Basin,
CHISWICK,
London, W.4.

My Ref: Fl/AW/MB.

Dear Sir,

I wish to record the disrespectful behaviour, and absolute disregard of orders issued by the Harbour Master, Harwich, against the Skipper of the Sailing Barge "VENTA" at 1030 on the morning of the 8th. instant.

He anchored in the Fairway between Harwich and Parkeston Quay: when requested by the Coxswain, who was acting under my orders, to shift clear of the Fairway and anchor on the north shore and to the eastward of the lightships, he became abusive. I went off to him myself: he was by this time "under weigh"; I told him he must anchor clear of the Fairway and he was very unco-operative and would not anchor where he was ordered to anchor.

I came ashore determined to order a Tug to anchor the vessel if he anchored in or near the Fairway, but he proceeded up the River Stour and was therefore clear of all shipping.

This Skipper infringed the Bye Laws of the Harwich Harbour Conservancy Board on two counts: - ONE, by anchoring in the Fairway; TWO, by being abusive to an officer of the Harwich Harbour Conservancy Board.

I would request you to advise this Skipper to acquaint himself with these Bye Laws, two copies of which are enclosed, and to act as sensible seamen do when given orders by an officer of a Harbour Authority. I will take no further action in the matter, but, as owner of this vessel, I would ask you to deal with this Skipper in a manner consistent with these offences.

Yours faithfully,

A. Waters
Harbour Master.

John came into conflict with him and took command with "I am the Master of this vessel and I shall put her where her safety demands", straight out of a favourite film we loved to quote in which Alec Guinness playing the captain of an 18th century fighting ship when questioned says, very authoritatively, "Because I deem it necessary". Nicholas had an illustrious ancestor, another Nicholas Hardinge, who commanded a British frigate in 1808. A convoy of well laden English East Indiamen was sailing south in the Bay of Bengal when it became prey to the French 'Piedmontasi' for which it would have been a rich prize. However gallant captain Hardinge although out-manned and outgunned came to their rescue at great cost to himself and his men and his vessel but won the day. This exploit has been recorded in a book, 'The Long Fight' by D. A. Rayner. Captain Fairbrother had a plethora of very quotable commands and ran a very disciplined ship. Nicholas was a very good mimic and loved to accompany Adam Faith's latest rendering on the radio. If John was in hearing he would immediately switch off the radio and say, "that's quite enough of that Nicholas". It was strictly classical and especially opera which John enjoyed and which suited Vernon and I but was hard on Nicholas. Occasionally Nicholas and Tony would break out on their cornet and trombone to relieve their feelings. Any religious programmes were dismissed with "We don't need any God bothering". The sacred programme was the shipping forecast listened to religiously in silence twice a day, as that was our lifeline.

10-7-64 1014 millibars. Moderate W. fresh wind at midnight. Left under all plain sail and set the bowsprit jib before we were clear of Beach End buoy at 1.10 a.m. shaped down to the Cork Lightship on the starboard gybe and thence off E. over the Shipwash sand which was quite lumpy. Gybed again and shaped for the Shipwash lightship. She didn't roll nearly so much on this gybe. Shipwash abreast 3.50 a.m. put the log over the stern, going very well with a slashing breeze. Our last view of England at sunrise was Sizewell nuclear power station. Called Nick at 6 p.m. having run 17 miles. Turned in until about 9.30 a.m. Everyone feeling the effects of being at sea, including VENTA.

Took over at midday having tried the pump about 1 p.m. it seemed the ship was making a lot of water 57 miles out, which the hand pumps with the addition of the motor pump were only slowly able to master. Fortunately Tony then found a bung for a hole which had been drilled to drain the fore hold when on the blocks. It had been forced out by the continuous movement. After its replacement things were much better, it was a nice sunny day and everyone was more cheerful.

There was not much wind now. Nick took over again at 7 p.m. until about 10 p.m. We seemed to be amongst the shipping routes. The faint loom of the Texel and the Den Helder light showed about 11.30 p.m. There was a bit more wind and still plenty of roll but nothing to harm. At midnight the log showed 99 miles with a speed over the last hour of 4¾ knots. Stemming the tide we only very slowly approached.

I had a nap until 3.30 a.m. when we gybed on to the starboard tack. It seemed very odd to turn in even for a few hours underway as this is something that has never been possible on the run from London to Harwich when there is always some change of course or sail trimming that needed both of the crew, so one only cat-napped on the cabin lockers, in easy call of the helmsman. I had never crossed the North Sea or any other sea for that matter till now.

11-7-64   1007 millibars. Strong S.W. wind. Rain. Passed two well-lighted offshore obstructions that may have been for drilling and numerous ships. Nick on again at 2 30 a.m. Called at 3.30 a.m. and gybed onto starboard tack as the light was coming up fast as it was after high water. Shaped in at E. Roared into Den Helder through the West Gat with breakers and dry sand each side. We followed a well buoyed channel then into the deep waters of the main channel.

The log now showed 123 miles. It seems to show very well. Took it in and after getting the jib down and anchor off the bow, made one board and brought up in a weather berth. Let go about 6.30 a.m.

Just got stowed up when a Dutch navy tug came after us and said we could not lay there as we would be aground at low water: he probably didn't realise we were flat bottomed. He towed us up and put us alongside in the yacht basin very carefully as the bowsprit was still down. At 8 a.m. a harbour official came up and asked us to sign the yacht visiting book which seemed to formalise our stay in Holland.

David from the Guardian went home about 10.30 a.m. Turned in and didn't wake until after 6 p.m. It blew and rained all day. After dinner about 10 p.m. Nick, Tony, David Pocknell and I went ashore to see the town which seemed to be very lively. Bought some smoked eels at a fun fair.

It was a beautiful starry night I noticed as we left England something which you can enjoy at sea. I went to bed but was conscious of the bumpy ride over the Shipwash and this part of the journey was not a comfortable one due to the weather we had had before we left. The barge rose and fell in the swell and pounded heavily down on the surface of the water as she was sailing light with no cargo or ballast. The crew had been aboard for some time and had gained their sea legs but the two Davids had a miserable time. They remained

Coming into Den Helder

on deck most of the night at the hand pumps. Vernon says he remembers me putting my head out of the hatch at one time and asking if anyone wanted a bowl of stew. There were no takers!

This crossing of the North Sea gave us one of the worst problems of the whole journey. We were using the hand pumps to pump out the incoming water and later the motor pump but making little headway. Finally Nicholas went to the skipper and asked should we not turn back as the water was filling the bilge faster than it could be pumped out. The skipper replied calmly, "Well we are half way across now so I think we had just as well keep going", and we did.

At 5 p.m. Tony found the fore hold bung floating in the bilge, forced in by the pounding movement of the barge. Hammered home, the problem was solved to everyone's relief.

It had been a very uncomfortable 30 hr. journey. Seasickness is a miserable thing. I am lucky in that I am almost immune, my mother also. Her father was a coastguard in peacetime and in the navy in the First World War and my grandmother's first home was a lighthouse on a rocky coast, so it must be in the genes.

On the return journey we hardly used the pumps. VENTA had been afloat then in Sweden for two years in tide-less waters and her hull was 'tight as a bell'. Before the outward journey VENTA had grounded twice a day on the Thames and elsewhere and had her bottom scraped and spiked at Chiswick. No wonder she was not at her most comfortable. The two Davids decided consequently to end their journey in Holland and David Fairhall who had suffered from seasickness worst of all, left that morning and we heard became Air Correspondent of the Guardian soon after!

12-7-64 Sunday 1012 millibars. Fresh wind. Rain coming finer and more northerly. Ashore, visited Naval Museum and the town with Nick and David posting letters and cards.

The crew of the tug ISSELL were very friendly and came aboard and we discussed our two countries at length, from the fact that our Prime Minister, Lord Home, looked rather ill to Socialism and the state of our health services. Den Helder was a nice, very clean, tidy and a well-run place in contrast to Parkstone. It is a large Naval base and we were surrounded by large grey ships which Queen Juliana was coming to inspect on Tuesday. Tony and I went to the Naval Museum which was also very clean and rather dull but later Vernon, Tony and I went out in the town to a local fair and that was far from dull. It reminded me of the English fairs I went to as a child before the war, very colourful and great fun. There were sweets, one of them 'Cupids Whispers' I had not seen since then and with the beautiful twisted brass columns and the blousy gipsy ladies it seemed like a scene from a Fellini film.

13-7-64 1000 millibars. Freshening N.N.E. wind. Bright sun all day. Calm at 4 a.m. Set topsail and cleared bob which had become fouled on the acorn by climbing up the topsail hoops. 9 a.m. finished starboard ratlines. Walked around the town. David Pocknell went back to London today.

14-7-64 1020 millibars. Light S.E. winds. 4.00 a.m. Pulled round to one of the yacht basin pier heads mooring up with slip ropes and set all the sails head to wind. With a bit of a heave from aft and a push off forward, she cast right away and just cleared the other pier head and at 5.30 a.m. made one board onto the starboard tack and shaped out of the harbour. In the light wind, progress was slow as we went out through the Molen Gat at 10 a.m. keeping a couple of miles off Texel. We had both the jib and staysail on the bowsprit and rigged a boom to lengthen the mizzen so as to set the Judge's sail as a mizzen staysail. With just enough wind to fill the sails the opportunity was taken to lower the boat and take some photographs showing VENTA in full sail.

During the day anyone steered who felt like it, we only divided up the night from 8 to 8 into something like watches. The wind came more from the S.E. so VENTA was close hauled on the starboard tack. Winded 7.30 p.m., head to the south, winded every 2 hours or so sometimes making good progress passing buoy E711 at 9.30 p.m. winded again.

At 9.50 p.m. and at 11.15 p.m. passed the Ameland light going well. Winded again to the S. There was so much phosphorescence in the water that when we brought up at H.W. 2 miles off Ameland in 5 fathoms at 2.30 a.m. and to the easterd of the lighthouse the anchor chain showed a great green light down into the water. The log read 35½.

Lovely morning with a nice breeze. Vernon and I hoisted a signal saying "Thank You". Hoping the harbour master in his tower saw it. The crew of the tug 'ISSELL were not around but an old boy cast us off who had told Nicholas how he had once on a visit to Hull been fined £5 for hitting a fish and chip shop proprietor. Nicholas was always so good at drawing out people wherever he went and whatever nationality. It was a gift which made him very good at capturing their personalities on film.

Outside the harbour we hit a tide mark of foam and strings of jellyfish which we had stirred up with our leeboard, more elaborate than the ones we saw on our East coast. I saw two quite magnificent ones with red frilly edges. Nicholas was on the wheel and told us of even more spectacular ones he had seen in Australian waters. Nicholas's father, who was managing director of Courage's Brewery at London Bridge, had wanted Nicholas on leaving Radley, one of England's foremost public schools, 'to go into the City'. Instead Nicholas had signed on as a steward on a liner taking '£10 Poms' to the Antipodes!

Off Texal we heard the guns announcing Queen Juliana's visit to Den Helder. I'm sure she would have liked to have seen us after all those grey battleships. Later we heard other guns from a firing range and Nicholas was upset at the thought of all that good brass scrap falling into the sea for often his two working barges had cargoes of scrap metal. We saw the Dutch navy out on exercise and further up the Frisian Islands the German navy torpedo boats rushed by just when we were so becalmed the tide was carrying us backwards. However it was a good opportunity to get off in the dinghy and take photographs of VENTA with all seven sails set and looking wonderful.

Help from the Judge's sail as a mizzen staysail

15-7-64   1022 millibars. Light variable winds. Underway 7.45 a.m. with a light fetching wind and the beginning of the East-setting tide. Boomed out Judge's staysail but soon gybed to get off the land. Picked up the Hubert Gat whistling buoy 12.30. Passed a large drilling rig 2 miles away in the heat haze somewhere in Freise Zeegat. Falling finer and finer. HW 4.30 p.m. Amongst channel buoys of the Ems used our large '*Seagull*' outboard to give her way enough to get to the N. of the channel and into about 5 fathoms so as to let go the anchor near the Geldsack Plate.

We spent the best part of three days off the island of Borkum without seeing it. We seemed in the middle of nowhere. There was no wind and the sun blazed down and there was even time to sunbathe. We heard on the radio that London had its hottest day for years. We had all the news and even 'Mrs Dale's Diary' and other reminders of home. There was a postal strike and I hoped my mother had received my card saying we had reached Holland. I never told her of anything of a rough passage and even so she worried far too much. Fishing boats came near one morning and waved and in the evening there was a lot of phosphorescence which even got into the kitchen sink somehow, both ghostly and fascinating.

We were all busy. It was good that we had enough water so that John could lower the leeboards and paint the hull behind them which we had never been able to do before. Nicholas put on some bow capping and Tony carved VENTA on the steering box sides, his forte. I did some painting and Vernon scrubbed around, it was good in such heat to keep the decks damp. We were getting smarter all the while with such talented hands. Vernon was getting agitated that two weeks of his three weeks holiday had gone by and we had not yet reached the Kiel Canal, but even he who was used to speedier sailing relaxed.

There were Dutch shrimpers all around. A pigeon stayed in the fore hatch for two days, we often have bird passengers resting aboard on their journeys. We once had a swallow on the bowsprit. I've never seen one not in flight before.

16-7-64   Next day was a total glass calm with heat haze and brilliant hot sun, We set the sails but never hove the anchor up. Everyone kept busy. I spliced the dolly line and got into the boat and painted that part of the barge's sides, inside the leeboards as they could now be lowered right down out of the way. We were still unable to see the shore and Borkum which was only 2 or 3 miles away. Visibility was only about 25 yards but we saw quite a number of ships.

17-7-64   1023 millibars. Coming moderate. Light N.E. Wind. Fine all day. Got underway about 10 a.m. Turned her off making about 4 boards winding up finally amongst the shipping about 4.00 p.m. Onto port tack, brought up at 8.30 p.m. after a short board off in 5 fathoms with what we take to be Juist ahead. The haze cleared and we saw Borkum quiet clearly and nearer than we had thought. We got underway again at L.W. about 11.30 p.m.

18-7-64   Nick and Tony taking her until 3 a.m. when we winded the ship, heaving up the weather leeboard and then Vernon and I took over and stood in for the shore again, passing back through the main shipping lanes. We made a couple more boards and brought up at 7.30 a.m. a mile or so due N. of Norderney.

Underway. Freshening E. Wind by 2 p.m. Sunny. Wind flew into S. with thunderstorm later. Care had to be taken that the windlass handles did not jump off the spindles as her head lifted when the chain was nearly short. There was a good slashing breeze and the old box came alive again, but going to windward in a barge at sea is not very good for a lady of her age and not all that much progress is made considering the effort involved. By the time we got to the Accumer Ee buoy at the east end of Nordeney there was too much swell for us to lie at anchor, so we followed the buoyed channel and got within ½ mile of a little harbour on the S.W. corner of Langeoog, bringing up at 7.30 p.m. Nick and I slid the bowsprit inboard before being called for dinner, as the spider band at the end seemed to be pulling back aboard. There was a great thunder-storm that night at 11 p.m. and the wind flew into the S.

19-7-64 Sunday. Called at 3 a.m. and made a board onto the land. Stood off again about 5.30 a.m. and made a board on again 6.30 a.m. Brought up off the town, west end of Nordeney 7.30 a.m. Underway again with more wind 2 p.m. Board to get the sails set and then off to the shipping lane and back. Another board off for ½ hour and back to the Accumear Ee buoy by 5.45 p.m. Followed the buoyed channel in and turned the last bit to just below the pier heads, the tide being then away 7.45 p.m. I think Vernon was disappointed that we didn't stay at sea and slog away as, to his mind, we had a fine large ship even though the motor pump was used every day and sometimes twice. Being used to smaller fast yachts he couldn't be expected to have the right patient attitude towards barges.

On Saturday evening we had an amazing storm. We were down below when a sudden strong whistling sound started up and we realised the noise was wind. It became overcast and a storm developed with thunder and lightning all around. Weather conditions are always more exaggerated at sea.

We were now in Germany and I, as flag officer, changed the courtesy flag accordingly. You could smell the sand and feel the wind hot off the land as we came near it. We must be very healthy by now with nothing but sea, sun and food for 5 days and quite warrant the Q flag we put out. Tony and I went into Langeoog harbour in the dinghy on Sunday but there was nothing open. We always liked to do our shopping in Holland when we were there, the food, the language and the courtesy are always a bonus.

I had worked for Agfacolor for ten years in the 50s and had applied to them for sponsorship with no response, so was interested in John's guests who came aboard having achieved it. It would have been useful but we did manage our journey with very little money, but lots of hard work and a tremendous amount of enthusiasm.

19-7-64 1013 millibars. Moderate S.W. wind. Bright at times. Nick got the bowsprit in order by putting another band on it first and putting a shackle in the bobstay. It was hove out again. A boat with the sail advertising 'Agfacolor' came alongside with an older man and three young couples, well cut, they came aboard and admired VENTA and shared their rum with us.

Underway 12.30 p.m. and made a few boards to the westward and then fetched out of the Zeegat to the Accumer Ee buoy. Set the log and pumped out and then gybed for the Wesser lightship with everything set and the Judge's staysail boomed out. Gybed again a mile before the lightship and passed it soon after 5 p.m. and then shaped N.E. for the Elbe No 1 lightship. The wind was falling finer all the time around high water with a ground swell rolling her from the W. At 8 p.m. the lightship was more than 5 miles ahead. It was nearly high water and with so little wind it would be impossible even to hold our position against the ebb tide. There was about 7 fathoms under us but the swell would make getting in the anchor, if we let it go, a hazardous job even to the extent of straining the bitheads. However the wind revived at 10.30 p.m. and we started to move through the water and picked up the lightship and with everything set, and the Judge set over the jib, we were making 7½ knots against the ebb and doing really well and were 4 miles to the E. of it by midnight.

The Elbe pilot boat came quite close and shone a searchlight all over the ship. I don't know what he thought we might be. 'The Flying Dutchman'? The phosphorescence was as bright as ever, enough to light the sides of the barge with green tints. We raced up the Elbe and there was no end of shipping underway, most of it bound up too, so most of our navigation consisted of following successive stern lights.

VENTA off The Frisian Islands

20-7-64 1017 millibars. Moderate W. wind. Falling finer. Passed Elbe No.2 lightship 1.40 a.m. and Elbe No.3 about 3.30 a.m. and at Cuxhaven beacon at 4.55 p.m. when it was light enough to take out our sidelights. We passed the two lightships, all with three masts so that they looked like old sailing ships. Logged up to 7½ knots through the water. As it came finer we got the bowsprit up just in time to bring up below the entrance to the canal, in about 10 fathoms.

The pilot boat came to us and then back with someone who could speak English. Nick, Tony and I went ashore and as none of us could speak German it was difficult to explain that we had quite a large sailing vessel with no engine. The authorities insisted that we must have an agent and that VENTA must be towed with a pilot aboard. Tugs were hard to come by but one was found and a price of DM1,000 was agreed. (VERONA had paid £10, with her engine.) The tug FALKE took us back to the barge and stayed alongside whilst we got the anchor up, which took some doing with 11 fathoms of good heavy chain.

Towed into the lock about 10.15 a.m. and out about 11 a.m. but we had only gone about 3 miles when one of the numerous traffic control stations had all its lights flashing red indicating we had to stop for large vessels coming the other way. The wait lasted four hours. A large ore carrier followed by R.M.S. ANDES (15,620 GT) passed, for which all traffic had stopped and then what seemed like half the French navy joined us in the lay-by. The tug master then decided he needed paying by the hour, so we all went ashore. It was illegal to leave a vessel in an international waterway, a free custom zone. The pilot came and made a fair amount of phone calls on our behalf until everything was sorted out and bought us all a beer in an old beer house. (As it happened the Kiel Pilots gave us an invaluable amount of service before they sent us on our way in the Baltic!)

Waiting for Royal Mail Lines ANDES to pass in the Kiel Canal.

R.M.S. ANDES. Length 643 ft,
25,676 gross tons, speed 21 knots.

Cuxhaven.
Entrance to the Kiel Canal.

I spent the time in the Kiel Canal dipping our ensign on the mizzen mast as a salute and receiving response from the French navy and others. We were a novelty as a sailing ship and looking so impressive and ship-shape too. The ANDES towered above us. When the price for the dues and the pilot and the tow were finally arranged we were set to continue but the £100 was much more than we expected on our limited budget. You were not normally allowed to sail through the canal but the wind being favourable and the pilot enjoying being in charge of a sailing vessel allowed us to set the mainsail and topsail and all the other passing pilots jokingly called out to him . We passed another S.S. VENTA .

20-7-64 Started again about 4 p.m. Went under two high level bridges and through a part where the canal was cut out of higher land with people fishing and sunbathing and windmills everywhere. The pilot pointed out a stork atop a tree. Got to Rensburg by 9.15 p.m. Towing had to stop at 9.30 p.m. before dark. Moored at the end of the commercial jetty.

Vernon had to go to hospital to get a wire splinter from the shrouds removed from his eye.

21-7-64 1015 millibars. Light N.E. Wind. Sunny. Turned out at 5.30 a.m. to be away 6 a.m. but there was thick mist and we couldn't see to the end of VENTA. The tug returned at 7 a.m. After the mist cleared, the weather came bright and hot with a light draught from the N.E. We towed on to Keil and straight into the lock with other small craft, mostly oil tankers. There was a change of pilots in the lock and we found we had the chief pilot, who had taken the opportunity to get out of his office. The tug took us out of the lock at 11.10 a.m. and we started to set sail but there was very little wind The pilot hailed the pilot boat which towed us down about 2½ miles down Kiel Bay with the chief chatting all the time in his perfect English.

Touched the anchor outside Laboe's small harbour full of yachts. The pilot boat went in to see if there was room for us, then came out and towed us to the main quay at 7.30 p.m. clearing other vessels away to give us the best berth, next the quayside. It felt rather odd to be afloat in saltwater and not have to tend mooring ropes because there was no tide. It was a perfect holiday day with a blue bay and with thousands of yachts sailing everywhere. A Dutch yacht came alongside about 7 p.m. The pilots' official charge was about 20DM but there was no charge for the tow and all the attention; including the chief pilot's arrangement with the Laboe pilot station to tow us out next day free of charge. There is a windmill in the town that is thatched from top to bottom. Also in the harbour is a marvellous lifeboat which has a smaller one on a slipway at its stern that can be launched when its parent vessel is doing 25 knots.

The chief pilot was obviously curious to see this rare vessel and took us to a favourite resort, Laboe. The only drawback to this berth was that this was a holiday town and holiday makers were so curious, we ate our dinner with heads peering down the hatch watching us at our meal! They wanted to know where the 15 crew members were. We all went ashore for a look around. The holiday makers created elaborate pitches on the beach where they surrounded their small plots with embankments and decorated them with shells which could be bought in the local shops. They sat inside in woven willow chairs. When the beach was empty that night the embankments had some damage done to them in retaliation for the Germans in the 1940s bombing and destroying Tony's family home in Poplar, in the East End of London and killing their cat, 'Binkie'.

22-7-64 1013 millibars. Calm, overcast and damp W. wind. Took on water in the morning. Shopped for cards and fishing hooks. Vernon left. The pilot boat towed us at noon out into the channel, where we set the sails but there was hardly any wind. There came a breeze from the W. about a mile to the north of the large naval war memorial. Passed the Kiel lightship 2.15 p.m., got the bobstay down having lowered the bowsprit almost at once after the pilot let go, with the log showing 3¾ miles with the wind increasing all the time.

Navigation aboard VENTA was simple, compass and log, dead reckoning with the occasional vertical sextant angle and compass bearing. In this part of the Baltic there are buoys every few miles marking the swept channels, though fishermen seem to go everywhere.

Shaped about N.E. by E. from there along the buoyed route. Shaped nearly E. at No.4 whistle buoy 4 p.m. Ran 8½ knots for the next hour with a rapidly rising swell. No.5 buoy at 4.55 p.m. and No. 5a at 5.35 p.m. Ran on 2 more miles and gybed at 32 miles on the log. Slacked the sprit off too soon and nearly lost it on a roll, gybed back and held it then back again. Tony and I got the rolling vang out. Topsail stayed down and mainsail still half up from 4.30 p.m. onwards. The mizzen was not set but the foresail and jib were. We had to sweat to heave the sprit aboard with the crab winch even with its much reduced sail area. We gybed on to the starboard tack without trouble; so that she wouldn't gybe too much I slacked the starboard vang fall, but too soon, with the swell now well on that quarter threatening to unship the boat from the davits, she rolled the sprit aboard before the lads had had time to get the rolling vangs in. When it rolled outboard again I thought "this is it, something is sure to go" but it didn't. I had only slacked it very little and the sprit end could only roll about 10 ft.

After this we gybed back onto the port vang which was tight in and this put the barge stern on the swell again so that she was comfortable. We ran on a little while like this until we had rigged the end of the port rolling vang fall to lead to a winch, then we gybed back without trouble as the sprit was hove right in the middle of the barge. We were then able to heave on the rolling vang and slack with caution on the vang fall, so all was well.

Passed Puttgarden buoy at the N.E. corner of the island of Fehmarn. Shaped in nearly S. and brought up in the comfortable lee of the island at 7.39 p.m. about a mile or so along its Eastern shore in 4½ fathoms about ½ mile off the shore and well in sight of the signal station at Marienleuchte. When we hauled in the trailing log at 7 to 6 p.m. it showed 39¾, an average speed of 8.2 knots from Kiel lightship. The log showed that at about 5 p.m. VENTA was running at 9.75 knots for 40 minutes. Dropped our topsail sheet in and made all snug for the night. There was enough current setting to the S.E.. to keep our head 2 points to the wind at midnight. Could see the lights of Lolland The sky was clearing with many stars.

There was quite a bit of roll running through the Fehmarn Belt and fanning out so that it was broad on our starboard beam as we lay head to wind. If anyone had not got used to the motion of the sea by now, by the time this little breeze finished, they would have. We rolled our guts out all the next day and the weather didn't come fine until the evening of the following day.

23-7-64

I thought before this evening that the land-bound, almost tide-less Baltic Sea would be a 'pond'. I didn't then have my present encyclopaedia which states: - "THE BALTIC: Tides hardly perceptible. Its weather treacherous and navigation is dangerous"! So it proved on this night. However Thor must have noted our golden acorn or perhaps we should thank our skipper who had made the decision to run back to the German island of Fehmarn to a safe anchorage. It was the fastest speed I ever experienced on the VENTA. It was exhilarating.

Off Fehmarn. Averaged 9¾ knots

Off Fehmarn.

23-7-64 1014 millibars. Moderate freshening W. wind. Dull, long showers. Laid at anchor all day. It began to look better about 4 p.m. and had been finer during the day but was blowing again by 6 p.m. with a small swell making the barge roll as it was right on her beam at 90 degrees to the wind. It was the swell from the Fehmarn Belt and a good indication as to the conditions at sea. As our next leg is at least 35 miles, it needs to be right to go. The gale warning black ball by day and red light by night are still on the signal mast at Marienleuchte.

24-7-64 1017 millibars. Still fresh W to W.N.W. wind. Gale warning still up. Lay all day. Fined away after about 7 p.m. and was a beautiful night the wind falling to a gentle breeze still from the W. and a great full moon showing land and sea like a black and silver etching.

25-7-64 1018 millibars. Light S.W. wind. Sunny. Underway by 4.45 a.m. and were soon head to the E. 6 a.m. Everything was set and boomed out that could be set. The sun shone, everything was perfect no swell at all except from passing ships and hot cocoa on deck to help us on the way. A small German coaster made two circles round us to take photographs about 11 a.m. and left us with lots of waving and horn blowing. During the day everyone who felt like it steered. We were reduced to our crew of four now and we began two hour watches at the wheel.

Picked up the buoys on E. by S. and the Gedser Rev lightship 12.45 p.m. 29 miles. Gybed there and ran 10 miles on port gybe to buoy R Gp FL2 4.20 p.m. Gybed again and set the Judge's sail again. Caught a mackerel also fouled the log line with the other fishing line. Sorted it out in ½ hour and lost about 2 miles or less on the log. The tackle cost me DM14 and I only won 8 Guilders from Nick.

Whis Wag 55 buoy 8 p.m. Ran 10 miles to the next by 10 15 p.m. Log showed 58¼. A bit more wind now. Passed last minefield buoy about midnight with 67 miles on the log.

Nicholas questioned whether the skipper could catch a fish with a simple line and bait. John caught a mackerel this morning and took it below and set it flapping in Nicholas's bed with him in it and then cooked it for his breakfast. No attempt was made to catch more as he had proved his point. The skipper had tied a large black pudding to the mizzen stay at the beginning of our journey and usually cut off a piece of that each morning for his breakfast. This was probably a very practical bargeman's tradition from a time before refrigeration.

26-7-64 Sunday 1017 millibars. Light S.W. wind. Fog midday. Bright sun. Gybed at 2.30 a.m. at 78 miles and ran on same course 60 degrees N.E. on the compass. It was quite fine with a fair wind making about 4 knots so that it was quite easy to steer and when necessary, leave the wheel to see that the sidelights burnt bright and clear or look under the mainsail. It was good to be quiet with just the barge and the cold black sea. There seemed to be no phosphorescence in the Baltic. When I was called about 2 a.m. just the two of us gybed on the starboard tack, between then and daylight it gradually came thick so that the colours of the sidelights shone out on the mist. Visibility was very poor. The Sandhaven siren could be heard just after 10 a.m. Ran on. When log showed 111½ miles gybed and put her on the port tack, wind abeam 10 degrees N.W. at 11 a.m.

Coming thicker but the bob was in bright sun above and the wind which was right abeam held fair and all sail was drawing and we were making good headway. We decided to try our lead line of 25 fathoms and I took about half of it right to the bluff of the port bow. A barge's lead is always cast from the port quarter, as the boat is the other side. The end is always made fast on one of the mizzen shrouds. Made a cast from forward with Nicholas to see it went free of the leeboard and I was able to walk aft and reel it in the usual way on the quarter. There was no bottom at 20 fathoms. We tried again every 20 minutes or so until about 2 p.m., we found 9 fathoms with Sandhaven about 2 miles to the N.W.

Liner W. of us, at 2 p.m. saw one ship at anchor and another small wooden one in a clear patch not more than 500 yards away. Could see their masts but not their hulls, it cleared a little and we saw the land abreast of us, about a mile away. Bore up, that is away from the wind, an expression that is a survival from tiller barges, and steered parallel with the land. 40 degrees N.E., 124 on the log.

Clearing all the time now. Passed Skillinge 3.30 p.m. and hauled in the log at 128 as we reckoned on anchoring near Simrishamn about 5 miles on, but then decided to continue as the weather seemed settled, across the bay to Utklipporna lighthouse 55 miles to the N.E. on off-lying islets. Gybed onto the starboard gybe and set the Judge's staysail. Boomed out and reset the log. Fell very fine by 9 p.m., but we were still going. Log which was reset shows 16¾ miles but at this slow speed, around 3 knots, it will under register by as much as 10%. Gybed at midnight onto port gybe. Took in the Judge's staysail as it tends to obscure the side light. Our second night underway was without event. Nick took over at 2 a.m. and I was called by Tony at 6 a.m. with 29 miles on the log and calm from N.E. Headed off about S. by E. and had 31 on the log at 8.30 a.m.

27-7-64

By now we were too far east to hear the English shipping forecasts and couldn't understand any Swedish ones.

Off Simrishamn in poor visibility before any sight of Sweden we smelt her, there was a distinct smell of pine trees. Nicholas who had experience of the Surrey Docks in London where timber is landed, said he had thought Sweden might run out of wood on seeing the vast quantities they exported but that was before he travelled across the country by train and saw their endless pine forests.

Our first sight of Sweden was unbelievable. The barge was enveloped in a thick white sea mist which reached to the top of the mast whilst the topmast was in bright sunlight with a blue sky. We saw a line of masts which we took to be yachts but we saw later it was the line of flagpoles belonging to the houses on the shoreline. Houses in Sweden invariably have a flagpole in their garden and the attractive national flag is hoisted daily whereas our Union Jack is only rarely seen in England to celebrate Royal events and to mark the end of hostilities. In fact in international London it was considered racist to do so until the 2012 celebrations. St George's flag however was seen at every football fan's window whether there was anything to celebrate or not.

Into the Baltic Sea. A 'cauliflower' round VENTA's head.

27-7-64   1009 millibars. Variable winds mostly from N.E. continued until 2 a.m. Handed over to Nick with very little wind and 27¾ miles on log. When Tony called me at 6 a.m. Got her off head to the S.E. 10 degrees. Winded to N.E. 10 degrees 8.30 a.m. 31 miles. Winded back on port tack 11.15 a.m. 41 miles and dropped jib and topsail soon after S.E. 20 degrees. Finer again at 2.00 p.m. After pumping out, dropped jib aboard and put staysail on stem to make her hold a better wind. Winded 3 p.m. 51 miles on the starboard tack. Laid up. 62 N.E. bright and sunny. At 4.30 p.m. wind went right around the compass in about 2 minutes with some very warm gusts and all the while there were great thunder clouds to the S.W. We lay about 65 degrees N.E. on the port tack 55 miles at 5 p.m. and 58 at 6 p.m. with the wind heading us to 80 degrees N.E. that is nearly E. The mainland was about 20 miles to the north of us and not visible.

Winded again at 7 p.m. We all had after supper, coffee at the table together, with a hand bearing compass for a tell-tale, while VENTA sailed herself. According to our progress on the chart we should have picked up the light of Utklipporna about 9 p.m. when it was dark. Going on deck to make a minor adjustment to the wheel the light showed clear in the right place, on the starboard bow at 9.15 p.m. Winded again 10.45 p.m. dropping the staysail down. All evening thunderstorms had been building up in the S.W. Still a light breeze but variable in direction. Called the boys out at 11 30 p.m. There was a thunderstorm nearly over our head. Hove half the mainsail up and down topsail, sprit almost in the middle.

Terrific thunderstorm, but after all our preparations not much wind. The rain came shortly after hissing across the water to us. By then there was almost continuous lightning and thunder and it seemed impossible that at sea with an 80 ft., mast it could not be struck as we were in the middle of the storm. There was even then, little wind and although it did puff from odd directions, we were virtually becalmed before the storm had passed on again over to the N.E. at about 1.30 a.m.

Again Thor had recognised our golden acorn! Or maybe it was our lucky horseshoe.

28-7-64 1004 millibars. Variable at first, freshening from the S.W. to S. Bright sun. Made sail again about 2 a.m., several more boards and were about 1½ miles to S.E. of the lighthouse. Nick was at the wheel when the wind came light from the direction we wanted, the S.S.W. about 8.30 a.m., after another mild thunderstorm. It freshened and we gybed with care because of the swell about 10.30 a.m. More wind until we were doing about 7 knots up Kalmar Sund, foaming along with the sun as hot as can be. After such a depressing night everything was wonderful.

Passed the whistling buoy 12.30 p.m. with 100 on the log and we had dropped the staysail and set the jib. Passed Utgrunden lighthouse 2.45 p.m., 113 ½ log. Hauled log at 128½ about 2 miles S. of Kalmar. Jib off, bobstay up, mainsail nearly up. The channel is very narrow amongst spar buoys and little islets. Just held our gybe and fetched the few hundred yards from the Sund channel to the harbour entrance. Let go in the large warehouse surrounded harbour because the bowsprit is still down with the foresail backed, got her close enough to the wharf to get a line ashore in the boat.

Moored up on Elevator Quay by piles of sawn wood, near a flour mill. There was a large audience, even the newspaper showed up. The police and customs came. After dinner went for a walk around Kalmar. It seems like a very nice old walled town.

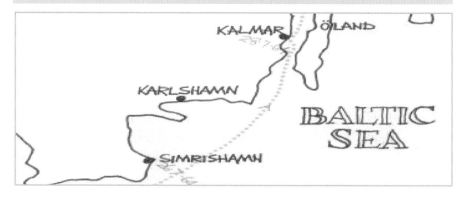

Resting before Kalmar Castle.

This was our first landfall in Sweden and a great introduction. We had seen its attractive castle on the rise when we were out at sea and John thought it looked an interesting place to visit. He negotiated an impressive entrance into the harbour and we got a good welcome from quite a crowd gathered on the quay who unbeknown to us at the time, probably knew of our coming long before.

There was no fussy harbour master telling us we couldn't moor here as on Britain's East Coast where sailing barges are common. Axel Anderson from the local newspaper, 'Barometern', came aboard and he was an expert on English sailing barges!

Leaving Kalmar Quay

This appeared in the paper next day:

"SAILING BARGE UNIQUE VISITOR TO KALMAR

"Such an unusual vessel - unusual not only for Kalmar Sound but also for the whole of Sweden as an English sailing barge, now converted into a luxury yacht arrived in Kalmar Tuesday evening. The vessel is called the "VENTA" and is from London. She was built in 1893 and still has her original rig. Since she has no engine, she has sailed the whole way from England, destination Stockholm. She is leaving on Wednesday. VENTA reached Kalmar in one final lap from Brunnsbuttle. She has had good winds, southerly and south-westerly, except on Monday when she had to tack against a north easterly breeze with the help of leeboards. These vessels are flat bottomed and of very shallow draught (VENTA draws only ½ a fathom) which is why a board is lowered into the water on the leeside to work as a sort of external loose keel when sailing with the wind. On the tack, there is a vital question of raising the one leeboard and lowering the other at the exact moment so that the turn will not be impeded- a thing which can be quite tricky and require a good deal of precision and experience in both crew and Captain.

"TO SPEND THE WINTER IN SWEDEN

"She is a sturdy vessel, but not particularly fast, says Captain Fairbrother. She has behaved well on the North Sea crossing and in the Baltic."

Good thing I wasn't interviewed here! I don't seem to have experienced the absolute doddle of a journey described and would have started talking of 'adventures'.

"THE BARGE VERONA AN ARCHITECTS OFFICE

"The barge is owned by Miss Jocelyn Lukins from London, and has a crew of three. They hope to join with a sister barge Verona owned by Ralph Erskine, an architect well known in Sweden who has been here for many years. He has converted the VERONA into an office and in summertime he usually sails off with his staff into the Stockholm and Södermanland archipelagos, and during the winter lies near Drottningholm Palace just outside the capital. The VERONA however came to Sweden in 1955 under engine only.

"Axel Anderson told much more:-

"Between 1900 and 1902 four barges were built in Sweden for the English Timber Co. Three of the four were delivered to England and traded for Everard's until at least the end of the W.W.2. They were given the names of KENT, ESSEX, SUSSEX and MARQUERITE and were built and registered at Bergkvara on Öland. They sailed under the Swedish Flag for the crossing. KENT, spritsail rigged, loaded with timber at Drag and sailed under foresail and mainsail from Degerhamm in late December 1900. The Sprit broke in half in heavy seas. Captain Götherström got the broken spar on deck, folded the mainsail in half diagonally and made for the Kiel canal. After a tow to Cuxhaven he was icebound for a month but eventually sailed under triangular mainsail and foresail only for the Thames estuary and handed the barge over to E.T. Eberhard of the English Timber Co. at Everards, Greenhithe.

"Two of the barges ESSEX and MARQUERITE were then rigged as ketches with their sprits on deck. MARQUERITE is recorded as taking part in the Thames Sailing Barge Match of 1908 under that name and coming second but later being disqualified. MARQUERITE traded until 1952, ESSEX and KENT until after the Second World War.

"The fourth barge SUSSEX remained in Sweden, ketch rigged, and traded there. Loaded with cement she was lost in 1911 off the north of Öland in a snow storm. Her crew of three were lost with her and she was never recovered."

29-7-64 1009 millibars. Strong W. wind fining away. All of us went out about 12.30 and walked round to the castle. Picnicked to the S. of it and then went inside as it is a museum. Also went into a church which was spacious and light with a good-looking organ. I went out again and took a few photos and posted cards. We also recovered our register from the customs and had our passports stamped. We bought Swedish charts and spent some of the evening looking at them, they make a bargeman shudder!

Kalmar Cathedral font.

Kalmar Castle (or 'Shott')

On this day the BEATLES arrived in Stockholm for the first time to a tumultuous welcome. However we were big news at Kalmar.

30-7-64 Light N.W. wind. Sunny. Pulled up to the end of the quay and set the sails. Cast when the wind favoured but it became fluky under tall warehouses. Finished by anchoring once, taking boards in all directions and finally having to have half a mainsail up to get her to bear up and get out of the pier heads about 10.30 a.m.

More fluky winds in the fairway at first then settled down the sun shone and we made nice way with Judge's sail set as a foresail. Went N. up the sound passing Masknaggen lighthouse at 2.25 p.m., Sillåsen at 1 p.m., setting the log at Slottsbredan at 3.20 p.m., 10 miles and Dämman lighthouse at 5.40 a.m., 17¾ miles. Fetched into the mainland side about N.W. and past the islands of Vållöromp where we made a short board to avoid running into a calm, after which the wind came much more steadily. During the afternoon I spent an hour asleep in the bowsprit jib as it lay in the net. The wind was too fine to set it.

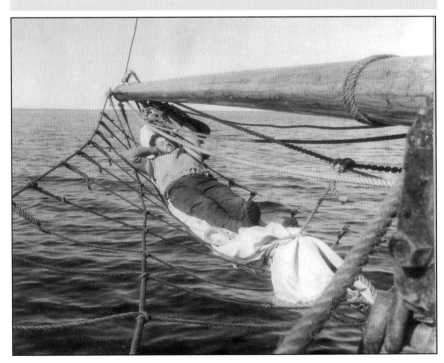

The Skipper resting under the bowsprit.

30-7-64   Passed small Täcktö and after two boards brought up in 7 fathoms, ½ a mile off the eastern shore of Rünno at 8.15 p.m. Lowered the boat and all went ashore in the nearly twilight having to paddle the last bit over the stones. Found wild strawberries ashore very small and sweet, back aboard by 9.45 p.m. to put up the riding light. A marvellous sunset sky over the pine wooded island.

31-7-64   1000 millibars. Moderate S. by W. Overcast. Underway by 4.45 a.m. Set course for the Blacken buoy with mainsail, topsail and Judge's staysail boomed out. Passed it 9.10 a.m. 18½ miles. It was dull sort of a day with the water quite clear but black under the overcast sky. On to Kungsgrundet lighthouse which we passed at 11.25 a.m., 32 miles. Gybed and set bowsprit jib and foresail. Innegrund buoy was passed 2.40 p.m., 49 miles. Gybed again to get off round some marks.

There seemed to be a lot of swell when our head was to the N.E. and again when Häradskär lighthouse was about 1.8 miles due N. Coming in a bit hazy. Found the channel leaving Sandö lighthouse on our starboard. The swell had increased when we cleared Öland. Instead of keeping at sea and sailing for Landsort some 50 miles to the N.E. where we had to go up a long inlet we had decided, with the aid of the Swedish charts, to try the inland passage amongst the islands. At times the channel was marked with a continuous black line passing places where it would be impossible to turn a barge. We left Håradsskår lighthouse to starboard and found the channel buoys, which are long vertical poles with spheres and up- or down-turned brooms. Ahead of us for some 3 miles there seemed to be nothing but small hills with no apparent opening.

However the only thing to do was to follow the compass and we passed more buoys and kept going. Rocks with the swell surging over them began to show on the starboard side. Shortly after, a tiny lighthouse like a

Chinaman dressed in white with a conical hat was seen marking the starboard side of the entrance to Sandö. I was mighty pleased to be out of the swell though it was by no means bad. We passed Sandö at 5 p.m. and hauled in log at 62 miles. We were at once surrounded by islands large and small, some no more than rounded lumps of red granite, others larger with crags and trees. It was necessary to keep the chart on the cabin slide well weighted to show the way.

There were numerous marks and a couple more small lighthouses that at night show green, white and red; you steer on white until you pass on to the white sector of the next one. We didn't do any night sailing! We covered another 7 miles and brought up in quite a large basin at 7 p.m. where the chart showed an anchor.

The second the last rope was coiled up, a fierce thunderstorm that had been threatening burst upon us. After it was over we went ashore, found some raspberries and climbed to the top of the island perhaps 160 feet high so as to look down on VENTA in a circle of rocky islands.

1-8-64 995 millibars. Fresh variable winds between S.W. and N.W. Many heavy showers and prolonged rain. Underway about 5.30 a.m. with fair wind about S.W. but which freshened and worked round to the N.W. When we got just past St. Högh it seemed obvious that there was not room to turn the barge in the one bit of the channel lying N.W. with a fresh wind and heavy showers, so we came back and brought up about 7.30 a.m. at Örskär, an anchorage on W. side of the channel where another nice little anchorage appeared on the chart. It was a beautiful place to be so we went ashore and explored one of the islands.

We lit a fire, which was handy to keep us warm through the showers.

A picnic on an island. The VENTA in the background.

2-8-64 Sunday 1002 millibars. Moderate N.W. wind. Dull. Remained all day as it was impossible to get further along this channel with the wind as it was and it wouldn't be much good if we went back and out to sea. Went ashore about 3.30 p.m. on another island and lit a fire, we made tea and baked some spuds.

3-8-64 1007 millibars. Light N. falling fine coming S.E. veering S. by W. Sunny. Lay all day as the fair wind did not come until 5 p.m. Went with Tony in the boat to see a passage to the S.E. if the wind is N.W. in the morning. We explored the possibility of sailing out to sea through the Islands but there were large areas on the chart not fully surveyed.

4-8-64 1006 millibars. Light S. to S.E. wind. Sunny at times. Underway 4.15 a.m. and set the Judge's staysail. It was very fine so progress was not swift but we kept passing islands. Falling almost a calm through the narrows at Horvelsö. We continued and were to the S.E. of Arkö beacon at 10.15 a.m. and shortly after went through the narrows. If we had had sweeps we could have touched the rock on both sides.

Boomed out the Judge again and lost our way on the chart for ¼ of an hour just before passing the island of Logen until Nick spotted the small beacon on a rock and we were able to pick up the thread of the channel again. Continued at about N.E. 20 degrees and came into more open water and shaped for Oxelösund when it again fell very fine.

At 2.40 p.m. having made 21½ miles anchored in 4½ fathoms in a nice rocky sided, tree covered bay where opposite us, 300 yards away, great 14,000 ton ore ships loaded in less than a day.

Nick, Tony and I went ashore and looked at a very modern church and missed the shops. Met a bloke from Liverpool. Nick and I went ashore amongst the trees before supper.

5-8-64	1009 millibars. Fresh to strong N.W. wind coming finer and more northerly in the evening. Rain after 7.30 p.m.
5-8-64 **to** **15-8-64**	We stayed at that anchorage for the next 10 days with nothing but calms and light winds from the wrong direction. Lots of odd jobs were done and many books read including 'Reeds'.

Looking back I wonder why we stayed so long. The next chart was half the trouble; we had about 20 miles of open water nearly as far as Landsort, then back amongst islands and then up this long inlet, almost a fjord, with turns and channel intersections, several lighthouses with an unlimited number of light sectors, not the sort of place to try in the dark. Also there was no end of deep water so that nowhere that looked like a comfortable anchorage, not to mention some places shown on the chart as "Not to be sailed over in thunderstorms as there are mines which might go off under those conditions"! However we survived with trips ashore, once to the flicks and one day Nick and Tony got the old box underway and had a sail about to see the anchor was clear, which it was. We also had a go at scraping the weed off her sides which was growing like summer grass in the fresh water.

In the 10 days we were in Oxelösund I only went into the town one day to the cinema. It was a children's programme with Harold Lloyd and Mr Magoo but we were needing any diversion by this time. Nicholas and Tony had gone ashore on one occasion to a white tiled sterile establishment which was the nearest thing in Sweden to an English pub. John had not taken a fee for his services and had joined us for the experience, even giving up his job. Nicholas was discussing with Tony what John should be paid and put his head in his hands and shook it and said "Oh I don't know?" and the proprietor came over to him and said "You Drunk, Out!". At that time, before the global influx of today, Swedish custom prevailed. In the restaurants and in buses and trains, anywhere in public there was no animation. It was a good thing Nicholas went quietly and hadn't done his little dance to accompany the latest rock and roll hit which he was wont to do or they would have called the police. The partaking of alcohol in Sweden was a very serious affair.

Kalmar to Oxelösund. The First Rocks

In England before we left I had asked a friend I had in the Swedish navy for some help in planning the journey. He said "There are lighthouses all the way." This was true of course but by the time we reached the rocky shores with their thousands of islets they were set on rocks and were reduced in size to just a few feet high with their conical tops, the little 'Chinamen'. However Johan was right and they did finally lead us all the way to Stockholm. However John did have a nightmare one night and was heard to call out in his sleep, "It's showing white all round".

15-8-64   1010 millibars. S.W. wind falling fine. Sunny. At last the wind came off the shore. Underway by 4 a.m. with not much wind and everything was soon set. The Judge's staysail boomed out on the starboard side. Passed Grässkären lighthouse about 5 miles from Oxelösund at 6.20 a.m. Set the log N. off Hävringe at 7.20 a.m. It read 21¼ miles. Set the jib and hove the staysail to the bowsprit with the dolly line. Then came a little more wind from the S. Passed over a magnetic anomaly of + or - 60 degrees (!) which caused Tony to bear up for no reason and nearly gybe. There are several of these deviations in this part of the world but at least true N. and magnetic N. are in exactly the same direction. We also came to where the charts had warned of mines which might be activated by thunderstorms!

Passed a ball buoy at 10. 25 p.m. with 11 miles on the log and shaped for Landsort on a course E.N.E. When about 3 miles from the lighthouse we shaped due N. passing to the W. of two small islands saving a couple of miles. At 1.05 p.m. passed Bråtknösen rocks at 21 miles on the log and hauled it in. We now started to run up the fiord. Dropped the Judge in. At Kockelskär at 1.20 p.m., Fifång 2.13 p.m., Stenskär 3.05 p.m., Ängsholmetn 4.25 p.m. Set the Judge again, then wind was falling away. Some holiday-makers rowed round us no doubt wondering what was coming into their waters. After this we only just got through the narrows at Branddalsund and anchored 400 yards to the E. at 7.20 p.m. about 3 miles W.S.W. of the light. A chap who had talked to us from his yacht when we were nearly through the narrows before running out of wind, returned before we got through and gave us a plate of freshwater crayfish saying it was a Swedish custom in August.

16-8-64   Sunday 1010 millibars. Light S.W. wind. Got underway by 6.30 a.m. and got up the remaining 5 miles or so of the narrows by 9.20 a.m. Sailed gently alongside the quay at Södertälje Outhamn about a mile or so to the S. of the town. We hope we might find a tug tomorrow. The canal was impossible to sail through with high banks and it has a railway bridge which only opens at certain times.

We all went to the locks in town after tea and we found a chap who spoke English and told us that we might get a tug from the saw mills opposite where we lay. Later Nick, Tony and Jocelyn went to see the Beatles in a 'A Hard Day's Night' some of which had been made at Strand on the Green at Chiswick. I walked round and then went back aboard. Measured the mast, using sextant, made it 83'3" from acorn to water, 85'4" on Tony's plans.

A 'Strand on the Green' scene from *A Hard Day's Night*.

17-8-64   1011 millibars. Light N.W. wind coming moderate S.E. Sunny. Nick and Tony, after talking to the harbour master in the office on the quay, fixed up for the saw mill tug to tow us. Started at 9.25 a.m. so that we could be at the railway bridge at 9 40 a.m. when it would open. Towed through the locks which raised us 16′ to the great freshwater Lake of Mälaren and the road bridge opened for us with Tony signalling our approach with his trombone.

Tony signalling the approach.

Clear of the canal and in the narrows at Linasundet, there came a little breeze from the N.W. and the tug, with only 15 hp and one cylinder, could no longer make it ahead so turned back, our rudder just touching stones as we turned.

The saw mill tug.

A fishing boat friend was hailed by the tug master who was aboard us, so we turned again and he got us through with no trouble and towed us to anchor just S. of the island of Kilholm by 12.15 p.m. we paid 85 Krona, 25 of which was to go to the fisherman. They all came aboard for a whisky.

The wind shot round to the S.E. after lunch at 2 p.m. so we scrambled underway by 2.15 p.m. out into the broadening lake which was most beautiful, disappearing to the horizon in some directions, with several large islands and trees to every water's edge. A field with cows was as unusual as rocks in the Blackwater. We kept to the S. shore which gradually turned to the S.E. towards more narrows that we must pass. We were off Långhällsudde about 3.30 p.m., made about 12 boards and got to the anchorage at 6 p.m., about ½ mile to the west of the narrows and 100 yards or so off the S. shore of Lillön. Went ashore in the boat and climbed about 300 yards to the top where we could see the tall buildings of Stockholm 8 miles to the East.

By this point in the journey we were seeing people around. One man on a cliff top gesticulated madly to warn us we were running into shallow water not realising we drew so little. One story told by bargemen tells of the skipper asking the boy lookout up forward "is that gull swimming or walking?". Meaning if he was swimming there was enough water to continue sailing. We saw our first skinny-dipping by some girls on nearby rocks and the binoculars came out!

18-8-64 1000 millibars. Fresh S.E. wind. Got underway at 10 a.m. and tried to turn through the narrows but the wind was against us coming off the high land. If the land had been flat we could have just fetched through or turned as there was enough room, but the wind fluked and puffed, so our leeboards touched the ground as she wouldn't come round. Let go the anchor just to hold her, backed the foresail and had another go. Continued with this for about an hour and a half but made no progress so ran back to our anchorage at noon. We needed to continue our journey as Jocelyn's mother was due to arrive.

About 1 p.m. a tug appeared which belonged to the same firm as numerous ballast craft passing to and fro. She thought we needed assistance and agreed to tow us through the narrows at Kyrkfjärden for £6, as we had no Krona. From there we turned with a fresh wind against us. Had a bit of trouble getting past Kungshatt, a small island in Lake Mälaren where there is a copper hat on a pole at the top of a cliff as a memorial. It commemorates when a Swedish king escaped his enemies by getting down the cliff and only losing his hat. By this time we could see the tower blocks and spires of Stockholm. Ran up between Kärsön and the mainland and through Nockeby swing bridge at 7 p.m. after Tony again sounded his trombone as a signal. The bridge had a crowd of people on it. Went out into the lake and then made several boards to the S.E. which brought us to Drottningholm. (Queen's Islet). At 8.00 p.m. sailed right up alongside

VERONA very well with little wind, stowing the sail as we did. Ralph Erskine gave us a turn and then came aboard and yarned.

VENTA and VERONA at Drottningholm.

I remember my very first conversation with Ralph Erskine was full of references to our mutual experiences of the various kinds of wood-rot the barges suffered from and the beetles that infest these barges in May. Apparently he had had contacts on our route who had reported our progress to him for although we seemed to be in very sparsely populated country we were being observed and reported on. Many people in Stockholm have summer homes in the archipelago.

19-8-64 1000 millibars. Light S. wind. Rain most of the day. Nick and I moored up with a wire ashore forward and a small chain aft. Stowed foresail and staysail. Visited VERONA and Mr Erskine came aboard about 4 p.m. and asked us up to his house about 8 p.m., a fabulous modern one. Stayed until 12.30 listening to him.

19-8-64 1001 millibars. Light S.W. wind. Bright. Jocelyn's mother arrived this morning from England. I went with Nick about 3 p.m. into Stockholm to see the customs, walking through *Gamla Stan*, the old town, not much success at the customs, will have to return tomorrow. Found out about the opera house at Drottningholm.

Drottningholm Palace.

My mother was much travelled and had journeyed by boat and train to arrive in Stockholm the day after us although we had had no idea whether we would have arrived by then. Of course, in 1964 there were no mobile phones and she didn't even have a land line. We had kept in touch by post cards!

However the first taxi driver she approached at the station spoke English, had read of us in his newspaper and knew of our arrival and exactly where we were moored. We were news again.

The Nockeby Bridge.

21-8-64   Went to the customs walking through most of the town. They decided the VENTA must be inspected so I returned with them in a car. During the time they were aboard the police turned up to inspect passports. The customs were satisfied but said that they would keep the register which appears to be normal practice. Returned to town with them and they directed me to a ferry that would take me to the VASA. Met the others there and we viewed the ship that was still enveloped in water spray. Visited the museum containing some of the things found on board as well as seeing two ½ hour films about her raising. Returned aboard about 7 p.m.

The warship VASA breaks the surface.

VASA in its museum today.

22-8-64 1013 millibars. Fresh N.W. wind. Sun all day. The VERONA's gear had been neglected and had been down for a long time. We all started on it at 2 p.m. and had it up by 7 p.m. Working the head rope on when the mast was half up. Set the sail to have a look at it. Tidied up and got the fall off the windlass.

This evening I went alone to the opera, walking over to the 18th century theatre adjoining Drottningholm Palace and saw Handel's *Ariodante*. Overwhelming experience that could not be seen anywhere else in the world, as the whole thing is done exactly as it would have been in the mid-eighteenth century with all the original machinery backstage. To come out after and walk through the formal gardens and avenues of trees, with the lake and the effect of the full moon was worth the journey.

The Drottningholm Palace Theatre.

23-8-64 1014 millibars. Moderate N.W. wind. Hove VERONA's topmast up and sent Tony up on the staysail halyards to retrieve the topsail whip that parted the line holding it down. Nick bent the head stick on the topsail. I started putting a patch on the foot.

24-8-64 1005 millibars. Moderate S.W. wind. Rain after 6 p.m. Finished the topsail. Nick helped to dress it with a wax preparation.

We enjoyed a weekend sail to Björkö with quite a large party.

25-8-64 1012 millibars. Moderate to fresh N.W. wind. Cast from the VERONA about 8 a.m. and after we got clear turned up Mälaren. Ralph Erskine, his son and a friend joining VENTA's crew. Turned through the narrows between Dävensö and Svartsjö about 5 p.m. After passing Vrakarsundet set the Judge at the end of the bowsprit which we lowered early on and the jib was a great help turning. Squared away and ran down between Adelsö and Munsö. Anchored at Björkö on which there are Viking burial mounds about 7.30 p.m.

26-8-64 Sunday 1014 millibars. Moderate S. wind. Bright at first. We all went ashore about 7 a.m. to look at the Viking earthworks. Underway about 8 a.m. with a light breeze from the S. Put Mr Erskine ashore at the ferry on Munsö so that he might catch a bus back. Got bobstay down and set the jib. the Judge was already set. Dropped it through the narrows though set it later, but changed them both for the staysail. Made long and short boards most of the way. Turned up to VERONA but VENTA did not quite shoot there and we had to touch the anchor. Moored up by 7 p.m.

29-8-64 The VERONA needed a lot of attention from John who worked to make her ship-shape in the ten days before his departure for England where he had an even bigger task ahead to fit out his own barge KITTY for charter work.

The skipper departs for England.   The barge Kitty.

31-8-64 My mother left for England. After a month moored next to VERONA we moved VENTA and anchored off as we were uninvited guests at Drottningholm, the residence of the Royal family in Spring and Autumn. They had a much more formidable one in the centre of Stockholm. Back in England, Richard Dennis who had lodged on VENTA before we left and who I later worked for, was at Sotheby's at that time and working in the Oriental department. The King of Sweden, Gustaf Adolf VI, came in and Richard was showing him some Chinese pots in which he was interested. Richard asked the King if he had met his friends on the VENTA who were moored at the bottom of his garden. The King graciously said that he had not but he expected he would. Unfortunately we never did meet him but we enjoyed Drottningholm and its palace grounds, the opera house and the Canton, a group of cottages in the Chinese style, built in the eighteenth century, to house silk weavers when the formerly secret process was discovered. They were now desirable 'Grace and Favour' residences.

Mrs Erskine kindly made me very welcome and created a 'home from home' for me in a foreign land. Her two daughters, Jane and Karin became friends and came to work in England later when we were able to return some of the hospitality.

The Erskine house, Sweden.

Anchored off meant we had no electricity and were back to oil lamps. However it was a pleasant spot and the small dinghy trip ashore landed in an orchard which no one else seemed interested in. The King probably had other orchards. We had to be careful with our money until we got work so we supplemented our meals with apples. In England I used to be popular with the working barge community when I made a meat duff and invited them in for a meal and an evening aboard. Their crews would bring gifts of Tate & Lyle sugar and cleaning materials as supplied by their owners. In Sweden we had apple duff with variations such as a chocolate apple duff. When the Erskine architects visited, Nabe, from Japan, referred to them as 'heavy English puddings' for they had nothing like it in Sweden or Japan either. I am not much of a cook but these puddings were very popular. In my home village they were originally boiled in the washing 'copper'.

Sweden was very advanced and they already bought their groceries in supermarkets which had not appeared in Britain yet. I never found a source of suet in Sweden and my mother sent me packets of 'Atora' in her food parcels.

During the early days at Drottningholm Nicholas and Tony worked on the Erskine house and the adjoining architect's office which was not then finished. It was a complex designed by Ralph Erskine and is now a 'Heritage' site. The VERONA would remain as added office space but mainly for recreation in the future. Tony and Nicholas also worked on the outdoor space making a feature of the rocky outcrops. They laid out a compass pattern using large round pebbles and built a wooden walkway linking the office with the house. Ralph Erskine despite his international standing did not have enough work at the time to take on Tony so that he eventually got a job in an architectural practise in central Stockholm. He later worked for Erskine in Sweden and continued to work for him for many years when we returned to England; on a very large project in Newcastle, 'The Byker Wall' and a smaller one for Clare College, Cambridge. The office had a very international workforce with architects and students from Denmark, England, Japan, India, Germany and Switzerland.

A study group of forty architects came to visit the Erskine office on one occasion and also visited us and the thing which took most of their attention on board was a high Victorian coal scuttle with a panel decorated with some very blousy cabbage roses! Later a party of 30 architectural students visited and again the coal scuttle got a lot of attention.

I also had difficulty in getting a job. I had wanted to work in colour photography on a Swedish newspaper, which already used colour illustrations. I had used a colour process in England which meant I could replace ten printers. The newspaper unions were so strong in Fleet Street that this could not be tolerated, not to mention a woman employed! Things had not changed very much since Caxton's day and it was another twenty five years and the 'Battle of Wapping' before we had colour in our national newspapers. The unions were so strong only a no nonsense Australian could break them.

I applied to my connections in Bayer, Germany at Agfa, who I had worked for in London for ten years and this got me a position with 'Colorteknik', their representatives in Sweden.

10-1-65 I started work there in January. In March we had a works outing to 'Dagens Nyheter', the newspaper I had applied to and it made Fleet Street seem Dickensian.

The Dagens Nyheter Newspaper Building.

Another problem to be solved was a mooring for VENTA. Stockholm has 5000 islets with miles of shoreline but although Nicholas and I tramped around the city we couldn't find anyone who would take us. However the Erskines had some Swedish friends Barbro and Birger Birgersson at Nockeby which was just over the connecting bridge from Drottningholm and they spoke to a neighbour, Director Rahlen, who ran the laundry there and we had a very nice mooring on their property.

We had the interest of the boats passing through the road bridge and it was attractive with lots of wildlife around. We often took the dinghy out on the lake at the weekend and collected wood for our open fire. We shared the beach with a host of perky little pied wagtails. We were not charged rent so I made sure we gave them our laundry - the only time in my life I have ever had such a luxury. We were also allowed to use the works canteen in the evenings to watch television and I remember 'Z Cars' was a favourite. English programmes on TV in Sweden, as in their cinemas, carried Swedish subtitles so there were no language problems for us. In our early days in Sweden Tony took Swedish lessons whilst Nicholas was giving English lessons!

Colorteknik was very well situated for a short journey via the efficient Tunnelbana service, which was an overland railway which ran frequently on time and with enclosed shelters on stopping points and well heated coaches.

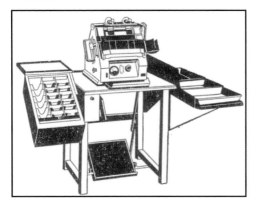

An Agfa Seriograph printer of the type used at Colorteknik.

My first job was on a colour printer turning out strings of amateur prints with just a few buttons to press to control the colour balance. This department closed down a month after I started there but I was retained and was transferred to the small unit which dealt with the work of professional photographers, fashion, cookery etc., all to a very high standard. We also had input from many other European countries that didn't have their own processing plants, as in the Baltic states. We also processed all the pornographic film from the countries such as England where it was illegal to send it through Her Majesty's Royal Mail and liable to confiscation.

There were only two of us in the unit and my boss was a very nice Norwegian, Germunde, which was a great bonus as they are a race with a similar outlook and sense of humour to the English. He could even enjoy the 'Private Eyes' Nicholas sent which were a great joy to me. Perhaps Sweden being

Jocelyn outside the Colorteknik building.

rather land-locked and in former times looking to eastern Europe gave them a different outlook. German was their second language until the Second World War. I made some very good Swedish friends at Colorteknik but we were an international workforce with very many from the Baltic States; one Englishman and a sprinkling of other nationalities. We all got on very well and everyone wanted to speak English so I never made much progress with my Swedish. I had about an hour's journey to work. Even the last walk from the station was pleasant.

VENTA iced-in.

In the first winter we had thick ice but very little snow and on the second there was very little ice because the snow fell early and remained for six months. It may have been sometimes down to -25 degrees but there is little of the combined wind and rain we have in England and the dry cold is much pleasanter and bearable. The factory was heated to 25 degrees inside so you shed a layer of outdoor clothes and worked in a comfortable temperature.

The day started with coffee and bullar (buns) in the canteen, very civilised. On gala days such as Lucia Day, December 12th, the start of Christmas festivities, the two Swedish directors sat down with the workers and provided a special feast with Glög, a hot spicy punch. I used the canteen in a neighbouring factory at lunchtime that served hot meals, usually with some form of sausage. Bacon was a special event but never a chop, meat was far too expensive. In the Colorteknik canteen everyone seemed to pay off their tab for the previous month in arrears. I paid as I went which was unusual.

I worked away in the darkroom loading frames with film and listening to music on the radio. One day I missed my lunch break as I couldn't bear to leave a performance of Tosca with Maria Callas. I must have worked at quite a pace as I worked alone and it made the time pass quickly. When I left Mr Jacobsen, my boss, said if I ever returned they would double my salary! He had agreed with Germunde that I was the best addition to that department they had had. However it was easy work for me as I had run my own laboratory working for Agfa in England. The higher salary would have been useful, but we managed very well.

Mr Jacobsen came to the VENTA once; everyone wanted to visit but needed a formal invitation. 'Call any Saturday or Sunday', as we would have said in England was not enough and a definite time had to be given. A gift 'for the house' was always brought on the first visit. We had lots of visitors as everyone wanted to see the VENTA. When a ship from the British navy came to Stockholm on a courtesy visit we even entertained two of their crew. Sveriges Radio came to interview us once and expressed surprise at us spending a winter on the VENTA but thanks to the very efficient Swedish 'Husqvarna' stove Tony installed, we were very cosy.

Whilst I was at Colorteknik there were two works outings. One was a boat trip to the island of Åland, off Finland. There is always a very fine Smörgåsbord table on Scandinavian ships. There was dancing but the main

VENTA cosy in winter.

occupation at any social gathering in Sweden, especially on the part of the boys, was to attempt to drink themselves 'under the table' as soon as possible. There was no draught beer as we knew it in England and the lager seemed very weak by our standards. Nicholas and Tony found it a very tame and expensive brew. However a very few glasses would have an amazing effect on the Swedes whose access to alcohol was very restricted. It was only for sale in government run outlets.

In Finland, my guest Tony and I went ashore hoping to do some shopping, but it was only a small town and the shops were closed. Finish design was very good. I liked Marimekko fabrics and both of us set ourselves up for life with 'Arabia' tableware which we bought at sale time in the big Stockholm stores. We did not have long ashore and only had a glimpse of Finland which was the usual Baltic rocky islets with pine trees. It was a good day out however and we all ate and drank and danced and met and talked with people from other departments. At the end of the trip the Finnish police on the boat were very roughly handling the heaps of bodies strewn around and I protested but they would not have understood even if I had spoken in Finnish. The Swedes too were very tough on drunks. If someone collapsed in the street, it was assumed they were drunk and could be very harshly treated; there were no 'Good Samaritans'.

The other works outing was to Gröna Lund, the fairground complex in Stockholm. Here I went on the big wheel for the only time in my life and suffered from vertigo. I could climb up rope ladders on the side of large ships in the Surrey Docks but not that. I insisted on Tony, Jane Erskine and I going to hear the French singer, Charles Trenet sing 'La Mer' in concert there, not quite their taste. They would have preferred to have seen a current pop star who was also performing that night, rather than Trenet at the end of his career.

There was not the opportunity to mix with my workmates on this occasion but I heard next day that at least three of them had spent the night in the police cells for being drunk and disorderly and I am sure their mates thought them very fine fellows. Whilst in Sweden I seemed to go to the cinema very frequently but of course the films were mainly English and American and it was a relief to experience the type of humour we missed. The Swedes as a nation took things rather seriously most of the time. I liked Swedish films but more so when I got back to England, with their subtitles and I could indulge my longings for Sweden.

A highlight was when we went to the University one evening and saw a cartoon programme which included Stan Hayward's 'Alf, Bill and Fred' which had been conceived on the barge at Chiswick. Two of the characters were originally based on Tony's dog and a mallard duckling named Fred we had then. Fred we removed from a cat's mouth one day and raised to maturity only to find we had to rename her Frederica. She adopted Stanley as a mother and spent much of the time using his sweater as a nest. She eventually realised she was a duck and swam off happily with a group of them. Stanley lived on VENTA for ten years and in his cabin there dreamed up a lot of the scenarios for his cartoons. Richard Williams of 'Roger Rabbit' fame was a friend and a constant visitor. John Halas of 'Halas & Batchelor' was a visitor once amongst many others from the world of animation.

Alf, Bill and Fred.

It was so good to see that programme, a remembrance of life before Sweden. At Stockholm Opera House I saw 'Tales of Hoffmann' but of course our local theatre at Drottningholm was the star where we saw Mozart's 'Cosi Fan Tutte' and 'The Magic Flute'. There we could view backstage and the amazing 18th century machinery. Elevated clouds which brought the gods down from heaven and rolling waves with a ship at sea were used in every possible production. Another highlight was hearing the architect Louis Kahn who had come to Stockholm on a lecture tour from the United States. Plenty of entertainment and lots of visitors. My diary at the time is bulging with occasions such as going to two parties in one night and dancing until 4 in the morning and driving back through a deserted Stockholm at sunrise. I'm not really a party person but the English fellows working in Sweden combined with the beautiful Swedish girls were a very strong mix and they seemed desperate to live in hectic style.

The English Rugger Club came to a party on the VENTA once and almost wrecked it. They were friends of Chris who crewed on VERONA. Some girl friends and I had a sewing circle which met sometimes on board, which suited my style. It was like sewing circles worldwide, an excuse for a good gossip and I could understand much of the Swedish 'girl talk' although I never learned to speak it. The vocabulary is much smaller than English and one word covers a lot of occasions. There was 'tack' for everything, for food when you finished a meal 'tack för maten'. Manners were important especially proper introductions. When you met someone new, you offered your handshake and clearly stated your full name, not as in England where introductions are so casual, it can be years before you discover a person's surname. In formal Sotheby's auction rooms in London when I became a dealer I was addressed for years as 'Jocelyn', as I knew them all so well as customers in the shop but they had never known my surname.

The first summer in Sweden, Tony and I were free to see more of the country. We went to Uppsala, a very interesting university city just a car **25-6-65** ride north of Stockholm. We did a long journey on a Swedish ketch from Göteburg. HULDA belonged to friends Ilhan Koman a Turkish sculptor and Kirsten his Swedish wife. It was their permanent home and they had small children. It was a spectacular journey going through the Göta Canal into Lake Vänern where I left as I was then at Colorteknik but Tony went through the whole 115 miles long canal and lake complex to Stockholm.

The Swedish ketch HULDA at Drottningholm.

When I went back to Stockholm in 2001, HULDA was moored at Drottningholm looking very smart indeed and I was told she belonged to Ilhan's son who was a toddler when I last saw him.

31-7-65 I also had weekend sails on VERONA and Tony crewed on her south to Kalmar once.

2-10-65 In October 1965 I went back to England for a month's holiday, travelling to Gothenburg by train and on to Tilbury, England by ferry boat. I stayed at Nicholas's flat in Gray's Inn Road and spent a month travelling around London as a tourist visiting friends and places such as our moorings at Chiswick, Faversham, West Mersea and Gravesend where everyone wanted to hear of our journey.

The two great differences between life in London and Stockholm were immediately apparent. First, the weather and how it was dealt with. I can't remember any time in Sweden when I was cold and our last winter in Sweden was the coldest in 30 years. Waiting for a bus at Butterwick bus depot at Hammersmith with cold wind blowing onto the waiting queue with only one side of glass protection, on the opposite side to the prevailing wind, it was absolutely freezing. Rain and wind, as experienced in England, is a bad combination. With the second difference England came out better. Traveling around London on buses and the Underground as a 'tourist' everyone was so friendly and complete strangers told me their whole life histories. Whereas we have improved our heating and comforts in public places since the 60s if you try to start up a conversation with your fellow travellers on public transport today you may well find they don't speak English.

In London I suffered from a bad throat from the pollution there after the clean air of Sweden. One evening Nicholas arranged a party for me at the flat and I remember it was the occasion when Richard Dennis found that the lavatory brush was sitting in an early Worcester bowl, and the rare item was given a new situation. Nicholas had inherited many wonderful things from the previous generations of Hardinges. Stanley took me to the National Film Theatre and John Vickers took me to the theatre. I shopped at Biba's store in Kensington High St. and visited Kensington Church St. and Portobello and the wealth of antiques which were there. I saw so many friends and of course my mother. It was a round of visits and occasions.

When I left from Tilbury my friend Margaret, Richard Dennis's sister, hoisted the Union Jack above her home on Windmill Hill, Gravesend on the banks of the Thames to signal 'Good Bye'. She came over and visited the VENTA in Stockholm in the Easter of 1966 just before we left and enjoyed it very much. She has lived much of her life in Shetland which seems more Scandinavian than it is Scottish. Earlier I had had a great send-off from my friends at Colorteknik and the 'Välkommen Tilbaka' was just as warm. My friend Eva's mother, Mrs Larson, had sent me off with a plant for my mother and gave me a big hug on my return. I was pleased to be back in Sweden. I don't think I ever felt homesick: I enjoyed both countries, especially my life in Sweden.

I settled back easily into my darkroom routine and even enjoyed the very hard winter and going to work at dawn. Of course we also had experienced in midsummer of reading a newspaper on deck at midnight, as daylight was continuous for a time. With snow on deck for six months that last winter the barge was quite cosy.

The VENTA in winter.

Condensation was a small problem in that VENTA's side decks had supporting iron beams on which icicles formed and we used to take a chipping hammer and a bucket at intervals and remove them. However the efficient Husqvarna stove kept the whole interior warm and our Swedish winter was more comfortable than one in England despite the lower temperatures. The condensation was probably caused by having water in the bilge.

6-11-65 Nicholas visited us for a weekend. He and Peter Light were on the east coast looking for a Swedish ketch suitable for Peter to use for charter work in England. One morning walking to work I saw a bush absolutely covered in a group of Waxwings eating the berries. They are very exotic and colourful birds. The majority of Swedish birds seemed to be birds of prey. The magpies were larger than the English version and glaringly black and white in the cleaner atmosphere.

Christmas in Sweden was beautiful. Houses were decorated for the enjoyment of passers-by with garden trees festooned with lights and curtains drawn back and windows again decorated with lights. The fact that most trees are pines and there are not the walls and hedges with which we surround our properties here, making an attractive natural landscape.

24-12-65 The main Christmas celebration in Sweden is on Christmas Eve. The traditional food was not all attractive. It began with a thin gruel of the water the ham was boiled in, 'Dopp i grytan', followed by 'Lut fisk' which was air dried cod with a strong smell of ammonia and considered a delicacy. This tradition must have reflected Sweden's past when most people lived and farmed in the country and food in the winter was scarce. Even in the sixties food could be rather bland without home grown vegetables. It must have changed yet again since refrigerated air transport has developed, bringing out of season vegetables from around the world. Christmas was very enjoyable and we spent Christmas Eve with the Birgerssons and Christmas

Day with the Erskines at Drottningholm, with their traditional English fare of a large joint of beef and Christmas Pudding. The only time I saw a joint of meat in Sweden was at the Erskines. On the third day we had an invitation to the Larssons. Eva is now a grandmother and we have visited each other and kept in touch through the years. Tony and I joined the Drottningholm group of carol singers and visited the Canton where we were invited in for Glögg and Pepparkakor and it became a very merry evening.

Our first New Year's Eve we spent in Stockholm at a friend's 9th floor flat at Solna which had a panoramic view over the city and we saw a spectacular show of fireworks from the height of the rockets.

Unique to Sweden are the millions of candles set at every window in the city. The candle industry in Sweden must be the largest in the world with most being handmade. The shops are always full of candles in every colour and shape. The next New Year we spent on the VENTA with a sparkler or two watching the fireworks displays over the city, sheltering in the hatchways for it was cold and later listened to the BBC and 'Auld Lang Syne' from England, which was run an hour later than the city's celebration due to the time difference.

1-1-66 Next day 6 inches of snow fell and that night the night temperature fell to -29 degrees, I think our coldest. We celebrated with chicken and a Christmas pudding sent by my mother and next day, Sunday, we had reindeer steaks, so we were enjoying the best of both countries. I went back to work on 5th January.

10-1-66 Tony started at the Erskine office and was able to ski to work. At Colorteknik we were given an extra coffee break on cold days. It wasn't of course cold inside just the management showing care. In the winter there was not so much film going through the plant and I was often allowed to leave early. A great proportion of the 35mm film in the summer was of course holiday 'snaps' and much of this was of the Canary Islands which must have become 'Little Sweden' in the summer months.

Everyone seemed very conscious of their short summers and in the canteen there were always rows of vitamin tablets beside their plates. Sweden had a fully comprehensive welfare system. I gave blood there as I had done in England and received 25 Kronor for doing so. It was arranged that all employees were to be seen by a doctor at intervals. I went along boasting my English health only to be told they had found an aberration in my heartbeat and I was not to over-exercise or carry heavy weights and to see my doctor as soon as I got back. This depressed me for in the next months I had to stock up the barge and arrange the preparations for our return journey. When I returned to England my doctor told me, I had always had this condition and "just forget it". The Swedish were always very thorough. Anyway we got on with our preparations. Tony had to repair the rudder which was on the shore. It had a lot of shakes in it and there was a lot of play which needed correcting as John had found on the journey out. We corresponded with Fred Cooper for advice and it was decided to have a metal collar made up to give strength to the rudder post and solve the problem that way. Tony designed the sleeve for the rudder and it was duly done at a cost of 500 Kronor and was a success.

The snow continued and there was a nice layer over the VENTA which kept us warm. There was always a 2 inch gap between the hull and the ice due to the heat of the interior and the ice was not very thick as the snow had come early. An ice breaker went through the bridge occasionally but most traffic had stopped. The central heating system in one of the large blocks of lakeside flats in Vällingby had broken down and it was a major news item with the shops selling out of electric and wood burning fires. My friend Eva had to take her boyfriend home with her as he lived in the affected block. I had visited there and it was heated by extracting heat from water taken from Lake Mälaren. I was pained to see the hot water tap was left running in the sink whilst we were eating our meal! The cost of heating and hot water must have been included in the rent. Living on a barge and having to fill the water tanks I've always used water very frugally even when on shore.

21-3-66 Nicholas arrived at the central station and walked around Gamla Stan and when I met him at the station later I found him rather gloomy saying he had been almost run down on the pavement in a car crash, and had seen enough of the town and that he wouldn't bother to come in again. He must have been tired or 'hung over' or suffering from shock. I tried to cheer him but as our

Gamla Stan in the snow and ice.

taxi left the station, a drunk collapsed over the bonnet and he said, "Now I know I'm Back!" Living and working so much together in the small confines of the barge you get to know one another very well and I knew he would soon be his usual entertaining self.

We used to make a joke about our 'years before the mast' being good for character building and hoping it was working. However Nicholas had come a bit early and with ice and snow still with us, a lot of work on deck couldn't be started.

23-3-66 Tony and I chipped the ice off the rudder which was on shore. We planned to leave on May 1st and I saw that my workmates questioned whether that would be possible, having more experience of the Swedish weather than I had. Vernon had early on explained that the seasons in Sweden are very different than our well defined ones. Winter can be long drawn out and Spring and Autumn can come suddenly and could be very short. I had found that when I had my holiday to England in October 1965; when I left leaves were just turning but when I returned in three weeks they had fallen altogether. The first sign of the end of winter came when a small bowl of coltsfoot appeared on the canteen table one morning. We would never think of cutting them in England; they consist of a yellow daisy type head on a brown spiky stalk with no leaves. Obviously they were well suited to be the first to force their way up through the snow.

Another harbinger of Spring is the Blåsippa which grows exclusively in the Baltic area and only in the south of Sweden.

Blåsippa Anemone Hepatica (photo by Eva Larson).

Colorteknik gave me a great send off, with many gifts and friends called at the VENTA through the next days. Ulla Kjellstrand gave me a length of material and a bag both woven by herself. Handcrafts were prized in Sweden. Jane Erskine gave me a recording of one of my favourite Swedish Folk singers, Sven Bertil Taube and there were many other gifts, it is a tradition the Swedes do very well. I had difficulty in reciprocating but did so with Victorian blue and white serving plates which Richard Dennis had given me to sell in Sweden but which I had never found the market for. Stoneware blacking bottles I had found in the mud at Lower Halstow, where sailing barges had brought them with cargoes of London 'rubbish' to the brickfield there in earlier days were a nice shape and appreciated too. Presents also came from a Finn, Gunitska, who owned ELSA moored near us who had become a friend and we gave him a Ventimeter, which measured wind force. Mrs Erskine baked a large container of fruit cakes, enough to last the journey. I don't think I have ever experienced such generosity and I am still quite overwhelmed in remembering.

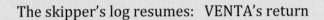

The skipper's log resumes: VENTA's return

16-4-66 Ron Hall drove me from Maldon to Tilbury landing stage to travel on S.S. BRITANNIA which was built in 1929, a single screw turbine vessel. We had time to look her over and admire the first class private rooms. She had a straight stem, low superstructure above the main deck, teak bridge and wheelhouse, a single funnel with the Swedish Lloyd star on it, two masts and an elegant counter stern. The most amazing thing about her was that when we stood on the landing stage, the only bit of her that touched the stage was the 5 or 6 inches of the overlap on one of the plate butts, from there she was either all bow or all stern. There were not two of her frames the same size. Bargemen will remember that she and her sister ship SEUSIA made the largest bow waves of all the ships in Sea Reach and below.

BRITANNIA eased off at 5.40 p.m. and almost at once took a 5 to 7 degrees list to port, a reaction to her single screw. Dinner was served soon after in the 3rd class dining room. In those days the meals were included in the ticket price. The pilot was dropped at the Sunk at 9.40 p.m.

17-4-66 Moderate to fresh N.E. wind and light snow showers. Danish shore lights were visible in the east by about 9 p.m. The ship berthed in Gothenburg at 6.30 a.m. After boiled eggs for breakfast aboard it was by bus to the railway station to take the express train to Stockholm arriving there just before midday. There was still much snow about on several of the many lakes we had passed on the journey, there had been men sitting by holes in the ice fishing. Nicholas met me and we took a taxi to the VENTA because I had a wood 'maids' box as well

18-4-66 as a kit bag with me. VENTA was lying only 3 miles west from the centre of Stockholm, in the large, island dotted fresh water lake Mälaren, surrounded by ice which came within an inch of her sides for she was well heated inside. A

small car drove by on the ice later that afternoon. The next 12 days were mostly bright except one night when there was 2½ inches of snow. The time was spent lowering down, varnishing mast and sprit, painting blocks and crosstrees, bending sails and heaving up with a new bob with the Hardinge arms. The biggest job had been the rudder, which had

been found on the outward trip to have had a badly split post, so that the yoke and the blade were seldom in proper alignment especially with the kicking strap in use. The rudder was ashore and Tony had designed and had a steel sleeve made up which when fitted solved the problem. A floating crane lifted the rudder back on the stern one morning. The top pin, which only just went below the second pin, was put in place. The bottom pin, about 18" long, and under very cold water, took quite a bit of juggling to get in place.

Nick and I went into central Stockholm to see the VASA again and collected the barge's register and did the paperwork we needed to leave.

Repairing the rudder.   Hoisting the rudder.

When my friend Margaret Stuart was staying with us at Easter she was amused at my going off to work one morning saying "I must find a crane to hire", something which would be very difficult in England. In Sweden with its thousands of islands and every other person a boat owner there were many cranes floating or otherwise and one came along very soon working on nearby Nockeby Bridge and the hire was quickly arranged for the equivalent of £24.

There was a positive attitude to a problem in Sweden which we don't always have in Britain. If there was a job to be done it was taken on even if they were dealing with an unfamiliar vessel like VENTA with no power of her own.

The crew consisted of Jocelyn, Tony Smith, Nicholas Hardinge and his life raft - without which he would never go to sea after losing his trading barge VERAVIA in the English channel on the 31st of October 1961 - and Brian Allen, 'Tub', who had crewed on the CENTAUR and MEMORY and had applied from England to come on the trip.

25-4-66 Tub arrived in Stockholm. The last to arrive were Jocelyn's friends, Caroline and Colin Banks and their 2 year old daughter Frances who were coming for a holiday trip

31-4-66 The Swedes celebrate at this time the arrival of Spring. That evening we all walked over the bridge to Drottningholm. There were large bonfires in the park, the evening finished with Jocelyn and friends drinking coffee in the China House kitchens, a royal folly in the palace grounds.

Ruth Erskine wrote to me a year later saying, "she would never forget our wonderful get off from Nockeby Bridge". There was certainly quite a crowd of friends. In the afternoon Herr and Fru Rahlen presented me with a large bouquet of flowers at the laundry and in return I gave them a very elaborate Victorian style brass lamp we had in the saloon which was a great success, with Fru Ralen almost in tears. We had never been able to exchange words as neither of us spoke each other's language and they had given us our beautiful mooring although we were complete strangers.

1-5-66 Wind moderate N.W. Sunny. We had decided a couple of days beforehand that we should try to reach Södertälje the first town south west of Stockholm by a different route to avoid some very difficult narrows which had caused a day's delay on the outward journey. At 8 a.m. we dolly-lined the 50 yards to Nockeby Bridge. There was no ice to be seen anywhere. We hove through the opened bridge, cast off from the knuckle of the old bridge and turned up the lake which laid N.W. and sailed on until we found our way was blocked by ice 4 inches thick. We were forced to return a little way, anchoring at 12 30 p.m. where Lake Mälaren was about a mile wide. We had good charts of the lake and in the Baltic that was needed; sailing without them would be impossible. Later quite a lot of ice drifted past us. A patrol helicopter came to watch our attempts to find a way through the ice.

2-5-66 Calm and Bright. At 11.30 a.m. sailed a couple of miles further into a larger part of the lake, only to find thick ice as far as it was possible to see, looking beautiful in the sunshine, so we returned again to the previous night's anchorage.

3-5-66 Sunshine and Light winds. We returned and anchored just clear of Nockeby Bridge! This could have been viewed as three wasted days, but not really as the conditions were unusual, as well as almost being a holiday for us. Some shopping was done and the bridge keeper agreed he would let us go through at 9.30 a.m. next morning.

4-5-66 Wind light S.W. Our large *Seagull* engine with the boat was enough to tow us through the bridge. We turned to windward all day. The wind in this arm of the lake was seldom true, as quite large cliffs came right to the water's edge, but there was enough depth for us to wind only yards from the shore. We anchored at 6 p.m. at Vallinge.

5-5-66 Wind E. Dull and damp. A fair wind through the narrows at Lillön that had caused us so much bother on the outward trip. There was almost no ice to be seen in this part of Lake Mälaren. We sailed to just north of Södertälje and touched anchor at 3 p.m. Long before, Jocelyn, Nick and Tony had gone ahead in the boat to find a tug. They returned at 5 p.m. with the same small tug as on the passage out, but she had by then a new engine. We towed into the short canal and locked a couple of feet down to sea level, dropped the topmast halfway down for the railway bridge below the town, then moored up at a sawmill wharf around 6 30 p.m. After dinner we walked back to Södertälje to get our passports stamped at the police station.

5-5-66 We enjoyed our sightseeing at Södertlje which had some interesting new architecture including a new town hall. I did more food shopping as I found a shop where they had reduced some of my favourite Swedish foods and bought some very nice decorative wall charts of sailing ships. I picked up some films from Germunde at the Post office and when I rang him he said his new assistant, Bertil, was not as fast as I was and I was missed. At the Pilot house

we found they had arranged for our previous tug and tug man to come for us and at 5 p.m. we towed through the lock and the narrows having struck the topmast. Barbro and Birger had left cards for us at the lock when they passed the Sunday before. We sailed to our old anchorage where we had had such a long wait on the outward journey, it all looked marvellous and it was amazing that this time the wind was favourable. We returned to the sawmill and the police station to get our passports stamped which at first they said was impossible but eventually the Immigration officer was persuaded to leave his television set and to come and deal with us. They obviously didn't have a lot of craft 'going foreign' from there and for some reason at one time they wanted to detain Tony! Back at the barge Caroline was entertaining the tug man and an English friend, Tommy Cooper, who worked at the sawmills and had brought his little boy to play with Frances. We gave him some colour supplements from the 'Observer' and 'Sunday Times' which I had always managed to buy, if a day late. Whenever the skipper was aboard we searched for his paper 'The Guardian'. The tug man gave me back half the 175 Kronor we had paid for his tow saying he had made a mistake!

6-5-66 Moderate N.E. wind coming fine. We turned out at 6 a.m. to find snow falling and settling. At 7 a.m. the tug towed us for fifteen minutes. We had a fair wind down the land-locked channel. After passing through Brandalssund, which required us to be nearly on the wind, we pulled up the boat in the davits, lowered the bowsprit and shortly had the jib and staysail set on it. We cleared the inlet south of Södertälje about 1.40 p.m. passing the last small lighthouse on its rock. The log already showed 16 nautical miles and we were making about 5 knots steering due S. We passed a lightship at 5.15 p.m., the log recording over 33 miles. There was now plenty of roll from the E. but the rolling vang was set up tight. The Hanadskar lighthouse was identified, several miles W. by S. of us distant on the mainland. It was 10 45 p.m. and our 54 miles on the log gave us a rough position. By 4 a.m. the wind had gone completely.

Calms from S. and E. from 4 a.m. to 11 a.m. came with fog, thick at times. The log was under-reading owing to our speed being less than 2 knots.

From midday a little draught from the E. gave us steerage way for our course due S. About 3 p.m. we could hear the siren on Kungsgrundet, a lighthouse on or near the mainland, which all down this coast has hundreds of outlying islands. Visibility was about two-thirds of a mile and at 4.25 p.m. the siren was judged to be due W. with the log reading 80½ miles, but chart measurement showed it to be 10 miles short. The fog eventually cleared at 7 p.m. and we could see to the S.E. by E. of us the light of the North Udde on the end of the large long island of Öland. By then there was a light southerly breeze. Steering W.S.W. we winded at the intersection of the red segments of lights on two small islands, giving us a position 2 miles N.E. of one of them, Fårö, (the home of Ingmar Bergman).

When night sailing, Jocelyn always made us tea about 10 p.m. The watch system started then, Nick with Tub, Tony with myself, and this lasted until breakfast time around 7.30 a.m. More tea was often made in the early hours of the morning. That particular night was one of the coldest I ever remember.

I learned very early on that sailing on a barge required tea being served at frequent intervals. I realised that running out of tea on this journey would have been disastrous. However, I was over-cautious and our stock of tea lasted the journey out, the two years we were in Sweden and for the return journey! It remained satisfactory and saved a considerable amount of money. Swedish food being twice as expensive as it was in England at the time and our many visitors who spent holidays with us were given a shopping list, whilst my mother sent food parcels all the while with items such as jelly cubes which were unobtainable in Sweden! Our desserts were always popular with our Swedish friends. However their ice cream was delicious and coming in from shopping after work I would leave the ice cream on deck when there was snow until needed for the meal. Refrigeration wasn't necessary.

Tony in Swedish army cold gear .

Sweden was way ahead of England in so many ways. Food was bought in supermarkets whereas in England there were still individual greengrocers and butchers etc. The supermarkets were of great help to me as my Swedish was almost non-existent but I soon mastered the names of foods and the supermarket checkouts didn't require much conversation.

The measurements being metric and my knowledge of supermarkets and the high prices put me way ahead when I returned to England where these changes were still ahead. Of course we enjoyed Swedish food and I still go to IKEA for a nostalgic meal from time to time.

8-5-66 Sunday Light southerly winds and sunshine. Still going, Nick and Tub took her towards Öland, winding at 3 a.m., a mile off the island's west shore. After daylight that morning I remember being on deck alone, close hauled on the port tack, with the wheel locked, I spent minutes on the bowsprit end whilst VENTA steered herself. This was an ability that previous skippers had remarked on when she was in trade. She was known for her ease of sailing 'on the chine' without the use of leeboards.

Tony and John changing staysail.

We were all day tacking to the south with the boards getting shorter, but still 4 or 5 miles each. We changed jib for staysail several times depending on which seemed to suit her best. The log was hauled at 4 p.m. and showed 151 miles. We had sailed the last 45 of them to make 25 over the ground. After several more boards, we anchored at 7.30 p.m. off Landskär, a small island on the mainland side of the Kalmar Sund, a third or more of the way through. The boat was lowered and we went ashore, having to wade several yards up the shallow stony beach. My log says, 'to get firewood and rocks for Nick'.

The weather was still very cold and was particularly bad for the Banks family who had probably been expecting a Spring holiday with more clement weather. We had also started to roll once we got onto the outside route and Colin and Caroline became seasick, although Frances remained bright. I managed to stave it off by taking it easy and only getting up to serve food which was mainly Swedish hard bread, very good in these conditions. The movement is always worse down below out of the fresh air and when you cannot anticipate the roll.

A cloud of small finches migrating north sheltered on the barge for a time three of them down below on my bedside shelf. Unfortunately none of them were saved and I had to brush up heaps of them on deck next day. I had recovered my appetite and ate a midnight night feast of salami sandwiches! We were going at a cracking pace sailing all night with our two efficient watches but missing landfalls we had hoped to make. With favourable winds one must take advantage of them when they occur. We didn't even see Gotland because of fog, a place I had hoped not only to see but make landfall. We had also hoped to do more shopping, not for food but for handicrafts. As it was, our last visit ashore was at Landskär, from where we came away with lots of Swedish souvenirs in the form of wood and rocks, for free! Nicholas had been painting a pet shop in Wimbledon before he left and knew the prices of decorative rocks for aquariums. John cut up loads of firewood. Tony found some setting booms and Colin a boulder for his garden. I found some heartsease a harbinger of Spring. Tony and I had a nice walk and watched a horned owl quite closely.

The boat made two heavily laden journeys with enough firewood for the whole trip and eight quid's worth of aquarium rock, which Nicholas delightedly stowed in his cabin.

9-5-66 Moderate to fresh N. wind. Fog at first. The fog cleared at about 9 a.m. We got the anchor up and made use of the fair wind, but it then shut in again to 500 yards. We brailed up the mainsail to the sprit, unhooking the main sheet block with the lowers in tight in case of a sudden need to gybe, then steered to keep a siren fine on the starboard bow. We had our foghorn in service, in case of other small ships being about. We passed the lighthouse with the siren, fairly soon, about 100 yards on the starboard side. Knowing exactly our position, the chart allowed us another 5 miles before the narrows opposite the town of Kalmar, where there is now a vast bridge between Öland and the mainland. We ran on for what we hoped was 4 miles and found a shallow spot, and let go in only 7 fathoms! That was quite a relief. We then all had lunch and ran through the narrows where there were no rocks, though the actual shores of the Sund were a mile away on either side. Gybed on to port gybe, pulled up the boat and made all sail, including booming out the Judge. The log was set passing a buoy at 3.45 p.m., at the next light tower, at 6.15 p.m. it showed 16 miles. We took in the Judge soon after and gybed again, running S.S.W. with more wind and swell, making 8 knots, we were soon clear of Kalmar Sund.

When we got to the corner where the Swedish coast runs east to west, we decided not to run on, but hauled the sheets and steered westward between the light of Utlängan on the mainland and one on an outlaying group of small islands by the name of Utklipporna, and there was much less swell having passed between them, the log recording 45 miles at 10 30 p.m. The distance between Utklipporna and Hällevik is about 36 nautical miles.

10-5-66 As is the way at sea, the wind nearly died about 1 a.m. It had started to rain at 11 p.m. and continued until 2 30 a.m. Tony and Tub had tried to keep her head W. by N. and the wind freshened again, so the topsail was dropped. Unfortunately it thrashed about developing a 3 ft rent under the head stick. It was an old sail. Nick and I had the watch from 4 a.m. and had found on the chart a small town with a suitable anchorage for a walk ashore. The wind moderated, still northerly, so the topsail was set again. By 9 30 a.m. we had made thirteen boards to get us to anchor 500 yards south of the Hällevik mole, the town being about halfway between Karlskrona and Simrishamn. It rained again from 11 a.m. to lunchtime, but the crew were turned in. We all walked ashore after lunch and some very good fish was bought for supper from a fisherman. They had rows of cod being air dried on supports. Later a fishing boat came out to us bringing a newspaper reporter and a photographer from the local paper.

11-5-66 Fresh wind E.N.E. Underway at 5.15 a.m. Set the jib and the log astern soon after, steering S. by W. across Hanö bay. We had heavy rain around 7 a.m. and then it came in hazy, with a big swell from the east, so much so that the un-breaking top of each swell came well above the horizon when VENTA was in a trough. Fortunately the fresh wind kept everything steady in that beam sea and we were making 5 knots. About midmorning we were not far off Simrishamn, unable to see it, but could plainly hear the fog signal. Soon after we were in the shipping lane and could hear several ships, one passed just visible at ¼ mile. We ran on passing the next headland, Sandhammaren, where it was thick fog, as it had been there on the journey out. I had thought of going round it to Ystad, and by 2.30 p.m. we had covered 44 miles.

There was a bit less wind by then but with 100 miles of clear water ahead, we kept going despite the fog. By 8.45 p.m. we had 67 miles under our belts, an average of 3½ knots. The midnight log showed 73 miles and there was very little wind. Ships lights were visible at about a mile, it was Jocelyn's job to kept our lights clean and burning bright.

We had a lot of fog on the journey south and although we had a foghorn we often used Tony and his trombone. I am not very happy being in fog in a relatively small wooden boat in shipping lanes. I spent a lot of time as lookout in the bow as shipping built up when we sailed further south to the Kattegatt and the Kiel canal.

Tony wards off ships in the fog with his trombone

12-5-66 Nick and Tony were on from midnight to 3 a.m. The log showing another 31 miles but with so little wind we knew it was probably under-reading again. Tub and I took over the watch and gradually a breeze from the S.S.W. came with the rising sun, backing slowly all day. We just saw in the sunny haze Dareer Ort lighthouse 21½ miles to the S.S.E. of us at 1.30 p.m. The log gave 116½ it having lost 7 miles. A sextant is most useful to find the angle subtended by a lighthouse whose height is marked on the chart; and just looking up the angle in Reed's tables to find the distance. We sighted the Gedster Rev lightships to the S. The Gedster is a headland on Denmark's most southerly island. With everything set, the wind right aft and the sun shining we were making 6 knots. We had to gybe a bit later to run westwards through the Fehmarn belt, and hauled the log at its western end at 9.20 p.m. and read 163 miles. We gybed again, stowed the jib and hauled the wind to anchor in 3 fathoms at 10.30 p.m. A mile from the west shore of Fehmarn, the German island.

13-5-66 We got underway at 6.30 a.m. and ran the 27 miles to the Kiel lightship in just perfect sunshine, fetched into the Kiel fiord bringing up at 2 p.m. just S. of the naval basin. I was surprised to see all the trees in full leaf, there were no leaves in England when I left and certainly none when we left Sweden. Jocelyn, Nick, and Tony went ashore for a little shopping and collected letters from poste restante.

14-5-66 Next day was still sunny, and a tow was arranged for the canal at 800DM but when the tug arrived he wanted DM1200, so we refused his services. Back ashore to the United Baltic agency, we were advised to return again on Monday. A German friend, Ewald came to call.

15-5-66 Colin and family left. We got underway after lunch and made three boards to shoot alongside the quay at the end of the old locks.

Caroline and Frances.   Frances, Caroline and Tub.

I hope Colin and Caroline enjoyed their holiday. It was not a leisurely one. John wanted quite rightly to take advantage of the favourable winds and he had a charter business to get back to. We had two good watches and took advantage of being able to sail day and night whilst Colin and Caroline kept to a normal time table. I should have realised the two were not compatible. Also there was the safety factor and the weather which as I've said before I had not fully considered. However Frances enjoyed herself and Caroline says it was a great experience when I spoke to her recently.

John found us a very nice anchorage off Kiel, in what Ewald told us was the 'snob' part. Caroline and I went into the ultra-smart Kiel Yacht Club to make phone calls. There were red ensigns on many of the boats for the forces of occupation still in evidence. We all enjoyed time ashore and booked Caroline and Frances's tickets on the ferry to Denmark next day, where she had some work at a museum. Colin returned to England. John, Nicholas and Tony went to arrange a tow for the canal. Tony and I had a nice walk in town. There was evidence of new building as Kiel had had a lot of damage in the war but it was all rather dull and the goods in the shops were all over patterned and tasteless after Sweden. Then we came on a shop window filled with garden gnomes!

It was now of course so much easier for me with only five of us and a strict timetable. Tony and I confessed that even in these first long sunny days we were missing the fresh air and landscape of Sweden. It was so fine I was able to paint the whole of the main cabin top and the rails in the next days.

16-5-66 We walked to the United Baltic and fixed another tug, United Baltic were very helpful and made no charge. There was a good ships chandler where we got more stores. The tug came for us at 1 p.m. and we went through the locks and left Kiel at 3 p.m. and locked out at Brunsbuttle at 10 30 p.m. that evening. We kept going in the dark although it was supposed not to be allowed and the tug man kindly towed us ½ mile clear of the locks to anchor in 10 fathoms, the Elbe is a deep river. The tugs charge was DM1232 including the canal dues. Everything continued to go smoother than on the journey out.

17-5-66 Moderate S.E. wind becoming less. Sunshine all day, flood tide all morning. Everyone else ashore 9 a.m. until noon. Nick buying several Prince Hendrik hats for himself and friends. Nick always wore one thereafter. At 1 p.m. stemmed the last of the flood and passed Cuxhaven at 3 30 p.m., No.2 Elbe lightship at 5 15 p.m., and made the low water just to the east of No. 1 lightship. Trailed the log there and sailed on the W. by S. to the Westerhill buoy, then S.W. by W. for the Wieser lightship which we reached at midnight, the log recording 21½ miles. The wind then failed and it was very sultry.

18-5-66 We dropped the topsail, hove up the mainsail because of a thunderstorm overhead, but no rain, squalls of warm wind from every direction. After all that we were 5 miles N.W. of the Wieser lightship with a light westerly breeze requiring us to turn to windward. By 9 a.m. there was less wind and thick fog.

19-5-66 At 12 15 p.m. we winded yet again heading S. by W., it was then an hour's ebb, which set us well to the westward. Later on we sighted the Norderney lighthouse, and after a few more short boards, brought up 2 miles N. of Norderney town at 5.15 p.m., the log showing 57 miles and the flood just making.

A Danish fishing boat manoeuvred alongside us at sea as we were sailing and generously tipped a basketful of codling and small plaice on deck. They asked us where we were from and where we were going and how old VENTA was and whether we had been to Denmark. Tub put a packet of

cigars in their basket but they made it plain they expected no payment. They said they were returning to Denmark in two days which as it happened was fortunate as this good weather we had been having, when I had been able to paint on deck each day, was about to break.

20-5-66 We had a very good supper and got underway again. at 10 p.m. just before high water and made 3 boards to the west to get the red segment of Norderney. Abreast the town, in the entrance at 4 a.m. and rolled about until low water at 9 30 a.m. then turned back to our previous anchorage which we reached in the hour. We lay at anchor all next day. Going ashore at 4 p.m. to look at conditions on the bar, there were no breakers.

21-5-66 By the following morning there was a fresh northerly wind. We had another go, underway at 3 a.m. when it was just daylight, but found too much short sea in the entrance at ebb tide to risk the sprit without the rolling vangs. Also VENTA's leeboard winches were well worn and the leeboards far from new of course. So it was back to anchor by 5 a.m.

22-5-66 Next day we lay at anchor as I could see the swell rolling in the entrance. Later we went ashore and walked along the front looking at the bar. I had just finished reading 'The Riddle of the Sands'.

I always had two copies of 'The Riddle of the Sands' in the ship's library and read it when we were wind bound at Norderney on two occasions. It is a 'rattling good yarn' set in the Frisian islands and written by an Irish writer, Erskine Childers in 1903.

Childers was a Sinn Fein politician who smuggled guns into Ireland for the Nationalist cause with his yacht and was shot for doing so in the Irish Free State in the Civil war of 1922! Shame! I always watch the film of the book when it comes around on TV. It stars Michael York who made a film on the VENTA on our return to our London mooring. He impressed me very much as he joined me over the side in the Thames mud. Mud-larking was a favourite pastime of mine, and I even made money with some of my finds. Michael always played rather aristocratic roles so he surprised me with his enthusiasm and not minding getting his shoes muddy.

We sheltered in the inside harbour at Norderney for 10 days in quite a spell of very rough weather. I couldn't stand on deck let alone paint there. We were anchored very near where the DULCIBELLA had been in 1903 and Norderney had not changed so much since then. The sands dried out and I would have loved to have explored them. We did make attempt one day but found we were in a bird sanctuary. The birds set up cries of alarm and we retreated. There were seals on the dunes. We turned our attention to the municipal dumps and found some souvenirs there before hurrying back for the weather forecast.

We went ashore twice and were able to renew John's black pudding. The German shopkeepers never let the language barrier stay in the way of a sale. In Sweden they were much more reticent. We bought some 'swine smalst' much to Nicholas's delight, he loved to air his attempts at languages. The holiday makers looked very frumpy after the immaculately turned out Swedes.

The rough weather raged on and one day force 10 was forecast and we registered 8 on deck on our 'Ventimeter.' The mainsail was chafing and John said if it had not been a new sail it would have been in ribbons after the amount of wind we had. It was difficult for all of us to sleep that night because of the rattle and roll. It was often sunny but the wind did not abate so I painted inside. We ventured to sea twice, at the first try there was too much wind but no roll, the second time there was too much roll but no wind and on the third time, Easter Sunday, there was quite enough of both but the wind was fair so off we went. I felt too seasick Sunday evening to get dinner when the saucepan somersaulted off the stove despite the fiddle rail! The barge seemed to be having an awful bashing. We didn't even stop at Den Helder where Nicholas had post and the tug IISSEL was expecting us by Whit Monday morning at 10 a.m. I was on deck again and it was very enjoyable and we were well on our way. It was the day of the Southend Barge Race. I couldn't even get excited at the prospect of getting home for the Blackwater one. I was still missing friends and Sweden. Getting back was rather an anti-climax and the end of an adventure. What next? I spent the afternoon on deck as it wasn't very pleasant down below.

I gave a bottle party in the fore hatch in the evening for Nicholas and Tony, having taken up possession of it again after having giving it up to the Banks family. John and Tub went to bed and left Nicholas and Tony at 2 a.m. to find the English coast.

By the time I got up they had found it and John was taking us down the familiar coast from Harwich. John said, "aren't you excited to get home?". I said I'd like to see Janet and soon after we passed SOLVIG, the Swedish ketch Peter and Janet had bought. It was looking very smart and I immediately perked up and I feel I must have had a premonition that I would go back to Sweden and buy a ketch; which I did two years later when I bought the SOLVIG's sister ship, the LUNA. Meanwhile we were nearing the end of VENTA's journey and safely back to Maldon.

29-5-66 Light to moderate Northerly wind and Sunny. Nordeney. We got underway on the high water at 6.30 in the morning. We had to turn to windward out of the entrance, but it was not as lumpy as before. Still rough enough to use the rolling vangs, even on short tacks, but just clear of the entrance we were able to fetch close hauled on the starboard tack along the Schulchter, W.N.W. with the ebb. There were breakers on the shallow water either side of us. Clear of the channel and in the small ship lane, sheets were freed and the jib set. During the days which followed the staysail was set above it and the Judge boomed out as the wind or our courage dictated.

30-5-66 We set the log at 9.05 a.m. off a water tower 2 or 3 miles to the south of the eastern end of Juist. We were north of Borkum lighthouse at 11.30 a.m. with the log reading 9½ miles. The Ems pilot ship came close to look at us around 2 p.m. VENTA passed due south of Terschelling lightship at 10 p.m., the log showing 65½ miles. The large swell from the N.E. had been with us since we had cleared Norderney. A nearly perfect day making 5 knots most of the time and a moonlit night.

31-5-66 The loom of the Texel lightship showed in the W. soon after midnight. Nick and Tony took over at 2 a.m. 2 or 3 miles N.W. of the Texel light. At 6 a.m. the log was giving 104½ miles and we then brought the wind to the starboard quarter, steering W.S.W. and settled down to sail straight for Suffolk. There was less swell and it was an altogether beautiful day. At 9.05 a.m. The log showed a 24 hour run of 121½ miles, by 1 p.m. 144 miles, by 6 p.m. 174 miles, by 7.30 p.m. 182 miles and by 9.00 p.m. 189 miles, the sun having just set.

Tony and Nick were hoping to pick up the Suffolk lights on their watch and Orfordness was sighted dead ahead at 10.20 p.m. With a moderate N. wind we spent most of the early morning stemming the ebb off Orfordness. However we passed the Cork lightship about low water at 5.10 a.m., having logged 233 miles. Off the Naze after 6.a.m., we hauled our sheets in a bit at the Knoll buoy. We hauled the log when off the Bradwell barrier wall at 9.05 a.m., 254 miles. Next we stove up the bowsprit and put the staysail on the stem when off Osea island. We fetched every reach and shot alongside the motor barge KING at Hythe Quay, Maldon. It was 10.45 a.m. English time, for we had put our clock back an hour off Bradwell. We were still on the same starboard tack at Maldon as the one we were on as we cleared the Sculcher Channel. There was still German mud on VENTA's anchor fluke.

I went to the customs, even went in *The Jolly Sailor* where dear Maud was landlady. Then it was back aboard for lunch and the start of telling our story to all the friends that had turned up to welcome us back.

At our first landfall in Sweden there was quite a crowd to greet us on the quay who had heard of our approach for some time and a local newspaper correspondent who was fully aware of the unique occasion of the arrival of a sailing barge making the journey from England under sail alone and with the spritsail rig. The approach to Maldon is always exciting for after a winding approach you turn the last bend to see the town rising above *The Jolly Sailor* with a charming little church behind and fronted by Hythe Quay, with its gathered barges.

Maldon with *The Jolly Sailor* fronted by Hythe Quay.

Sailing barges arriving on the tide at the quay is a common occurrence but one from Sweden unique. The local newspaper did interview us but, soon after MEMORY with her charismatic skipper, John Kemp, came in from a weekend sail to Southend minus his topmast and a topsail hanging in ribbons, that was much more newsworthy! We only had minor tear to our topsail after our 854 miles from Sweden and with no disasters to report we weren't really news!

However something momentous happened that day when our we passed through the door of the quayside hostelry. Home at last we celebrated our return in style at *The Jolly Sailor* with a great appreciation of English beer and the institution of the English pub.

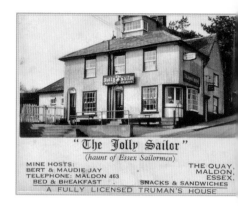

" The Jolly Sailor "
(haunt of Essex Sailormen)

MINE HOSTS:
BERT & MAUDIE JAY
TELEPHONE: MALDON 463
BED & BREAKFAST .

THE QUAY,
MALDON,
ESSEX.
SNACKS & SANDWICHES
A FULLY LICENSED TRUMAN'S HOUSE

I hope we toasted our Skipper John Fairbrother then. He was always in charge, appearing completely unflappable whatever weather, or problems that were thrown at him. The elements throughout our journey were obvious they were sometimes to our advantage but always to be respected. John's friend, barge skipper Peter Light, was once interviewed on Anglia Television. His interviewer, John Bassett, who owned the VENTURE said, "Skipper, do tell us the adventures you've had" Peter replied laconically, "Only idiots have adventures" and the interview almost came to an end. John was of the same persuasion and in barge parlance, 'he deserved a medal as big as a frying pan' for we had had the best of skippers who with all his experience had made that casual remark on Maldon Quay a reality and it had led to a unique journey under spritsail rig which could never be repeated with today's restrictions and given us all a great time to remember.